CW01215786

# QUAIL
## THEIR BREEDING AND MANAGEMENT

### G.E.S. ROBBINS.

This Edition published 1981 by the World Pheasant Association,
1 Harraton Square, Church Lane, Exning, Suffolk CB8 7HA, U.K.

© G.E.S. Robbins.

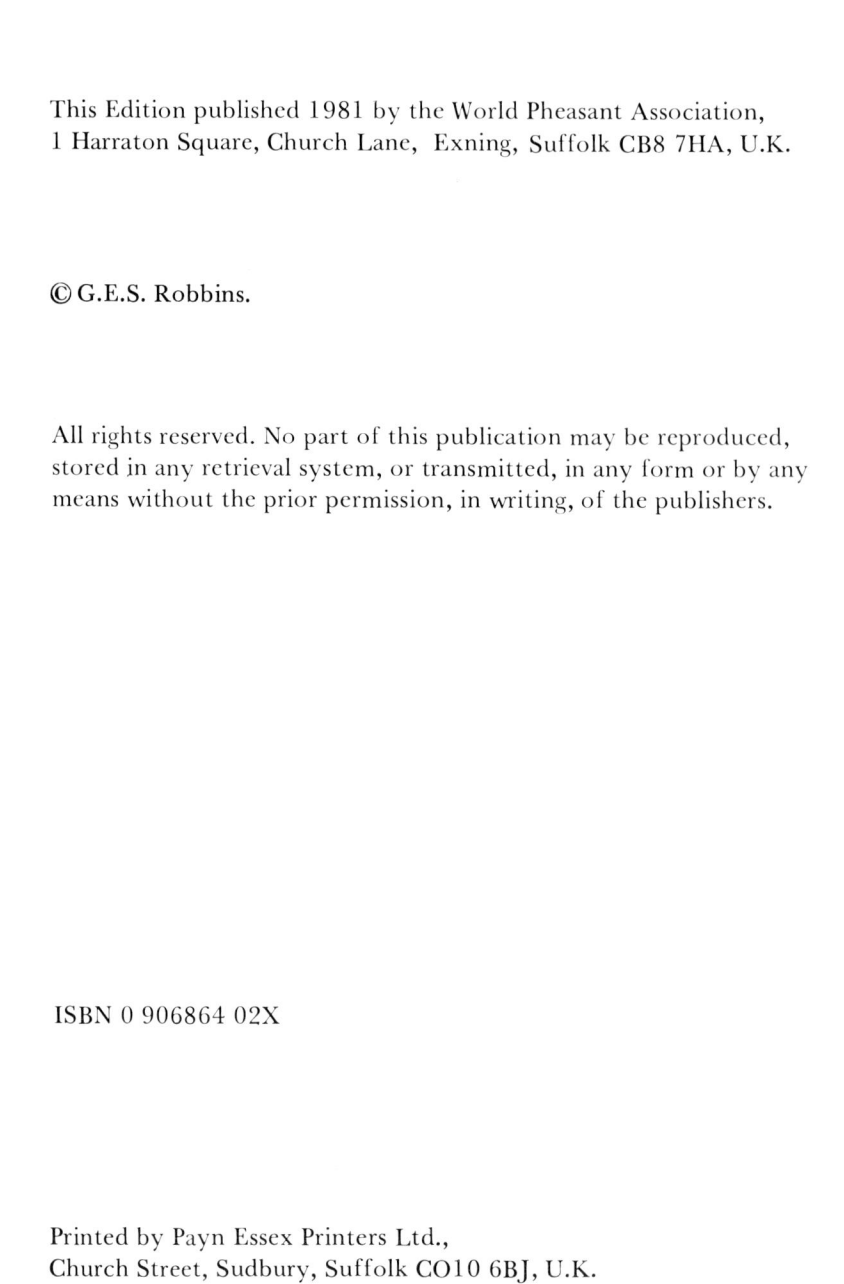

All rights reserved. No part of this publication may be reproduced, stored in any retrieval system, or transmitted, in any form or by any means without the prior permission, in writing, of the publishers.

ISBN 0 906864 02X

Printed by Payn Essex Printers Ltd.,
Church Street, Sudbury, Suffolk CO10 6BJ, U.K.

# CONTENTS

| Chapter | | | Page |
|---|---|---|---|
| | Acknowledgements | | 6 |
| | Preface | | 7 |
| 1 | Introduction | | 9 |
| 2 | Aviaries | Aviary selection | 11 |
| | | Space requirement | |
| | | Finance | |
| | | Existing facilities | |
| | | Accommodation | |
| | | Size | |
| | | Materials | |
| | | Netting | |
| | | Design 'A' Quail Breeder House | |
| | | Design 'B' Quail Pens | |
| | | Design 'C' Quail Aviaries | |
| | | Housing for less hardy species | |
| | | Catching birds | |
| | | Egg Collection | |
| 3 | General Management & Husbandry | | 19 |
| | Common Ailments | Infectious Sinusitis: Cause, signs, treatment | |
| | | Bronchitis & Pneumonia   ''      ''      '' | |
| | | Respiratory Disease     ''      ''      '' | |
| | | Enteritis               ''      ''      '' | |
| | | Blackhead               ''      ''      '' | |
| | | Coccidiosis             ''      ''      '' | |
| | | Scaly-leg               ''      ''      '' | |
| | | Lice & Mites            ''      ''      '' | |
| | | Newcastle Disease       ''      ''      '' | |
| | | Worms                   ''      ''      '' | |
| | | Vet's Advice | |
| | | Administration of medicine | |
| | | Disinfection | |
| 4 | Feeding | Modern Poultry foods | 23 |
| | | Chick diet | |
| | | Adult diet | |
| | | Live food | |
| | | Maggots, mealworms | |
| | | Grit | |
| | | Food Additives | |
| | | Minerals | |
| | | Vitamins | |

| | | | |
|---|---|---|---|
| 5 (a) | Quail Species | Species for the beginner | 27 |
| | | Purchase of stock | |
| 5 (b) | Check list of Quail | | 30 |
| 5:1 | | Bearded Tree Quail | |
| 5:2 | | Long-tailed Tree Quail | |
| 5:3 | | Buffy-crowned Tree Quail | |
| 5:4 | | Mountain Quail | |
| 5:5 | | Scaled Quail | |
| 5:6 | | California Quail | |
| 5:7 | | Gambel's Quail | |
| 5:8 | | Elegant Quail | |
| 5:9 | | Banded Quail | |
| 5:10 | | Bobwhite Quail | |
| 5:11 | | Black-throated Quail | |
| 5:12 | | Crested Bobwhite | |
| 5:13 | | Marbled Quail | |
| 5:14 | | Spot-winged Wood Quail | |
| 5:15 | | Rufous-fronted Wood Quail | |
| 5:16 | | Black-fronted Wood Quail | |
| 5:17 | | Dark-backed Wood Quail | |
| 5:18 | | Chestnut Wood Quail | |
| 5:19 | | Rufous-breasted Wood Quail | |
| 5:20 | | Gorgeted Wood Quail | |
| 5:21 | | Tacaruna Wood Quail | |
| 5:22 | | Venezuelan Wood Quail | |
| 5:23 | | White-throated Wood Quail | |
| 5:24 | | Stripe-faced Wood Quail | |
| 5:25 | | Starred Wood Quail | |
| 5:26 | | Spotted Wood Quail | |
| 5:27 | | Singing Quail | |
| 5:28 | | Mearns Quail | |
| 5:29 | | Ocellated Quail | |
| 5:30 | | Tawny-faced Quail | |
| 5:31 | | Eurasian Quail | |
| 5:32 | | Japanese Quail | |
| 5:33 | | Rain Quail | |
| 5:34 | | Harlequin Quail | |
| 5:35 | | Chinese Painted Quail | |
| 5:36 | | Pectoral Quail | |
| 5:37 | | New Zealand Quail | |
| 5:38 | | Brown Quail | |
| 5:39 | | Snow Mountain Quail | |
| 5:40 | | Indian Mountain Quail | |
| 5:41 | | Jungle Bush Quail | |
| 5:42 | | Rock Bush Quail | |
| 5:43 | | Painted Bush Quail | |
| 5:44 | | Manipur Bush Quail | |

| | | | |
|---|---|---|---|
| 6 | Breeding Requirements | Health | 86 |
| | | Nutrition | |
| | | Fertility | |
| | | Environment | |
| | | In-breeding | |
| | | Stress | |
| | | Stock | |
| | | Housing | |
| | | Conditions | |
| | | Laying season | |
| | | Egg eating | |
| | | Temperature | |
| | | Light | |
| | | Natural Food | |
| | | Keeping of Records | |
| | | Storage of Eggs | |
| | | Egg storage humidity | |
| | | Storage time | |
| | | Turning of Eggs | |
| | | Candling of Eggs | |
| | | Hatching by parents | |
| | | Hatching by bantam | |
| | | Sitting box | |
| | | Incubators | |
| | | Humidity Control | |
| | | Temperatures for Quail | |
| | | Siting of the Incubator | |
| | | High Temperature | |
| | | Low Temperature | |
| | | Pre-heating of Eggs | |
| | | Hatching by Incubator | |
| | | Brooders | |
| | | Floor covering | |
| | | Food & Water | |
| | | Brooding Temperature | |
| | | Alternative types of brooder | |
| | | Transfer to the outside | |
| | | Bantam rearing of Quail | |
| 7 | Quail at Liberty | | 102 |
| 8 | Importation & Export of Quail | | 103 |
| | | Quarantine Premises | |
| | | Endangered Species | |
| | | Transportation of Birds | |
| | | Shipping Documents | |
| | | Feeding & Watering | |
| | | Containers | |
| | | Design for Quail | |
| 9 | World Pheasant Association Quail Group | | 106 |
| | Bibliography | | 108 |

# ACKNOWLEDGEMENTS

To those people who have helped me over the years in the keeping of Quail, my thanks; in particular my colleagues in the World Pheasant Association, with their Chairman, Tim Lovel, Keith Howman, and Bill Thornhill, for their help and encouragement in writing this book; my special thanks to Thomas R. Warwick, who has given so much help and details of how Quail are raised in North America. My thanks also to my secretary, Olga Keveren, for the long hours of patient typing from the manuscript written in my minute handwriting.

However, particular thanks to my wife, Wendy, who has had to put up with many hours of my being shut away preparing this book and the general upheaval in our house.

*G.E.S. Robbins*

# PREFACE

I felt extremely honoured in being asked to write this book; my experience over the last eight years has principally been obtained through trial and error, and as there is still very little written on the subject of the management and breeding of Quail, I thought it would be helpful to the beginner if this book included all the information I looked for when first starting to keep these fascinating birds.

As with all types of aviculture, new ideas and techniques are being tried each breeding season, therefore, do not take this information as final, although the majority has been based on my own experience, be prepared to experiment yourself within reason.

Finally, I would like to wish readers of this book as much pleasure and satisfaction as I have had and continue to enjoy from keeping these delightful birds.

*G.E.S. Robbins*

8

# CHAPTER I

## INTRODUCTION

When one mentions the word quail, in most peoples minds it immediately brings a picture of a game bird prepared for the table, but in fact to those who have become involved in keeping these delightful birds, the thought no longer enters their heads. With the fourty-four species to choose from, the aviculturist is faced with a major challenge as there are only twenty-two species currently held in captivity (WPA Census 1978), all of which must be established into a sound breeding nucleus as an insurance for the future. Too much natural habitat is being taken in the world to feed and house the world population, therefore it is necessary to act now for the future. It is accepted that by holding birds in captivity they lose their natural traits, that is; defending themselves, eating natural foods etc., therefore the aviculturist must regard the birds as being in trust and maintain them in the best conditions possible, not allowing the birds to degenerate through breeding. The way in which your birds are housed and fed must reflect the environment from which they are found. For instance, the Mearns Quail *(Cyrtonyx montizumae)* must not be subjected to a damp, frosty climate, as they are found in the dry, hot area of Mexico; on the other hand, the European Quail *(Coturnix Coturnix)* must have protection from the roof of their house as at certain times of the year they have a migratory urge which compels them to move on, and if not protected they can kill themselves by dashing against the roof. These are just a few points that should be taken into consideration. Being the smallest of all the Galliformes, Quail represent a wide difference in size with the smallest being the Chinese Painted Quail *( E. chinensis )* being only 4½" long (102mm), to the largest, the Long tailed tree Quail *(Dendrortyx macroura)* 13½" long (330mm). A further contrast being the habitat, the Blue Scaled Quail *(Callipepla squamata)* from arid desert areas, to the Bearded Tree Quail *(Dendrortyx barbatus)* in high mountain forests, and the Spotted Wood Quail *(Odontophorus guttatus)* inhabiting tropical jungle. According to the last issue of the IUCN Red Data Book, only one species of Quail is considered endangered, the Masked Bob White *(C. V. ridgwayi)* that is not to say there are many more which are facing the possibility of dying out over the next few decades due to the destruction of their habitat, therefore we must take up the challenge as it is perhaps the one branch of aviculture where, for a small sum, a pair of birds can be bought and the offspring successfully reared. To keep healthy stock genetically sound requires a sizeable "genepool" and care should be taken on the part of the breeder (this will be outlined in later chapters) to ensure that pairs are from as widely dispersed genetic lines as possible. It requires many people in countries throughout the world to take up the hobby and it is hoped that the information in this book may encourage more to do so. One day *you* may be called upon to provide breeding stock for re-introduction into the wild.

# CHAPTER 2

## AVIARIES

### Aviary Selection

There are many types of housing used by the Aviculturist to keep his birds, and his choice is dictated by a number of basic things; space, finance and existing facilities. In addition there are the personal likes and dislikes of the individual as to whether he thinks his birds should be kept on wire, sand or a soil floor. We propose to develop each of these points mentioned to help the beginner to make his decision regarding the type of accomodation he requires.

### Space Requirement

Quail provide the aviculturist with the unique opportunity of keeping members of the Galliformes family without having to provide a large amount of space, as required by the larger species such as Pheasants, Grouse and Guans. The person who has only a small garden or backyard can easily accommodate six species of Quail within an area of 16' (4.9m) x 4'(1.2m), whereas the Pheasant breeder might only be able to house one pair of small Peacock Pheasants in such an area, therefore, having only a small plot available does not stop the keeping of these charming birds. One word of warning - certain species do have a perpetual call, particularly during the breeding season, which might upset the neighbours if they are housed too close.

### Finance

It remains with the individual to decide how much they are willing to spend. The size does fall within the scope for a "handyman" using new or secondhand materials. Of course, there are new houses manufactured and sold for small game birds and these can run into several hundreds of pounds each, being principally designed for the game bird farmer. Various types of housing will be discussed in more detail later in the book.

Existing facilities

Quail often appeal to the person who already keeps other birds, and use Quail to clean up the seed at the bottom of the aviary. One prime rule must be remembered - that adult pairs of Quail must not be housed together, or with any other member of the Galliformes, as they will fight, especially during the breeding season. Housing with other birds, such as Finches and Softbills can be very successful and utilises the floor space of the aviary. There are two major dislikes of the less hardy species of Quail, damp and draughts. These must be borne in mind when housing in an existing aviary. Suitable cover and a day area must be available at all times. There is a further consideration to be taken into account; certain species do perch, and will fly up to roost, thus disturbing the other occupants.

Accommodation

For the serious breeder of Quail, pairs should be housed on their own, so that their breeding performance can be recorded, eggs identified, and ailments kept to a minimum. The best possible accommodation should be provided for two reasons; an old structure of rusty wire on a secondhand frame does not enhance the occupants or provide the best environment for the birds to be kept in good health, and breed, apart from the need to undertake running repairs at regular intervals, which if not carried out, could result in a valuable bird being lost. In general, the Quail aviculturist will agree that money spent on a good design and long life materials is well worth the extra investment.

Size

There are a number of schools of thought as to the space required to house various species of Quail, and Aviculturists seem to have differing views in various parts of the world. In America, Quail are in general kept in small wire cages housed in a shed or similar building, with a total area some 4' (1.2m) x 2' (.6m), others house their stock in larger units 8' (2.5m) x 3' (.9m). My own preference is a house of approximately 4' (1.2m) x 4' (1.2m) 16 sq.ft. to accommodate a breeding pair, ensuring they are maintained in good condition. This requirement has been developed over a number of years, and has proved to be very satisfactory. Of course, the small Chinese Painted Quail do not require such a large area, 2' (1.6m) x 3' (.9m) is quite adequate.

## Materials

Suitable housing can be constructed from a variety of materials, timber, wire, galvanised, asbestos and polythene sheets.

## Netting

The first decision to make is to prevent sparrows and various other vermin from entering the houses, therefore the choice of the correct size of netting is important. Should the breeder decide to allow his stock to raise their own chicks, the wire size required must be very small, certainly less than ½" mesh (1.3cm), for general use ½" wire mesh will satisfy most requirements where a house is at floor level; also remember if your house does not have a wire bottom and is placed on the ground, the side should have wire mesh fixed and extended out around the edges of the house for at least 12" (.3m) to prevent vermin digging under the house, Quail are particularly vulnerable to such an attack.

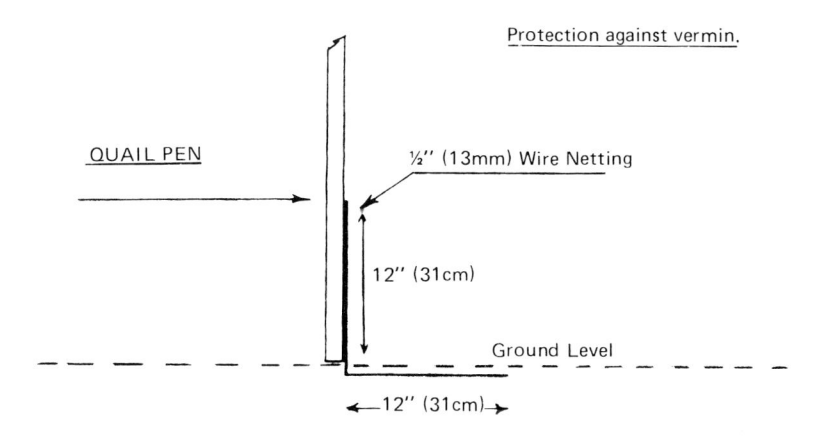

Protection against vermin.

QUAIL PEN

½" (13mm) Wire Netting

12" (31cm)

Ground Level

←—12" (31cm)—→

## DESIGN 'A'

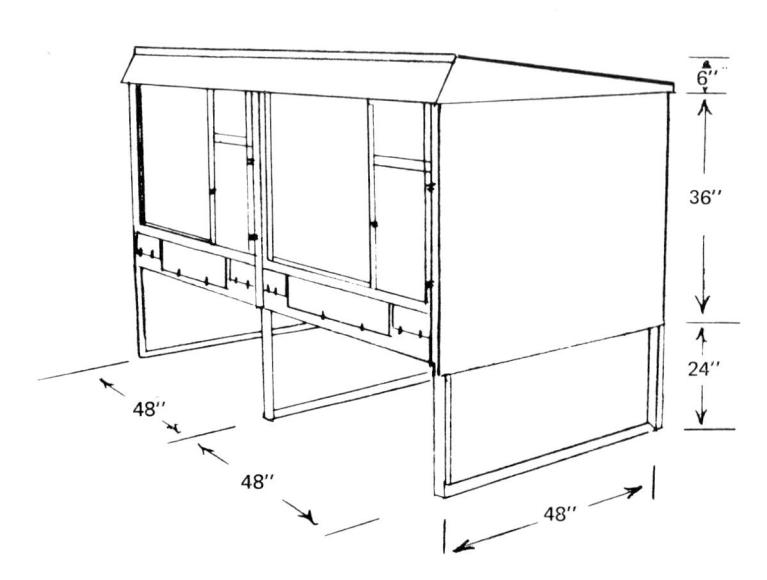

It is also suggested that to prevent sparrows entering the house the maximum mesh size should not be larger than ¾"(19mm), as they have an uncanny knack of finding their way in and consuming food, thereby leaving disease behind. The only slight disadvantage of such a mesh size is the aesthetic one of the wire being obtrusive; this can be reduced by the application of black bitumen paint on the galvanised wire, this type of paint can be easily applied by using a cheap foam decorating roller. Coating wire with black bitumen has the advantage of increasing its life, and allows one to see the birds more clearly. For those who wish to use traditional housing and require a mesh roof for the pen, it is advisable to use some heavy gauge black polythene garden netting or one of the terylene game nettings which are now available in a variety of gauges and mesh sizes. The advantage being that Quail are inclined to fly upwards when frightened, and can easily scalp themselves if galvanised wire is used.

Designs

Before starting aviary construction, it is important to decide on the species you propose to keep. The main consideration is whether the aviary is to house a species which is totally hardy, needing a good shelter, but no heat, or one that requires limited heat in order to survive the winter. There are a number of designs which the aviculturist might like to consider, depending on his needs.

*Design A - Quail Breeder House*

This house has been developed over a number of years, through trial and error, taking into account the basic requirements of the hardier species, using it as a breeding house and accommodation throughout the year. The house was designed as a module construction, which can be added to as and when required. The birds have plenty of light and air, but no draughts or dampness to contend with. The floor is covered with a mixture of sand and peat, which remains dry throughout the year, completely free from disease. The food and water can easily be replenished without upsetting the birds. In each side of the front of the house there is a small nest box, which has a bob hole to allow the birds to enter and lay. Access is also via a small door on the front to enable the eggs to be collected for artificial incubation.

## DESIGN 'B'

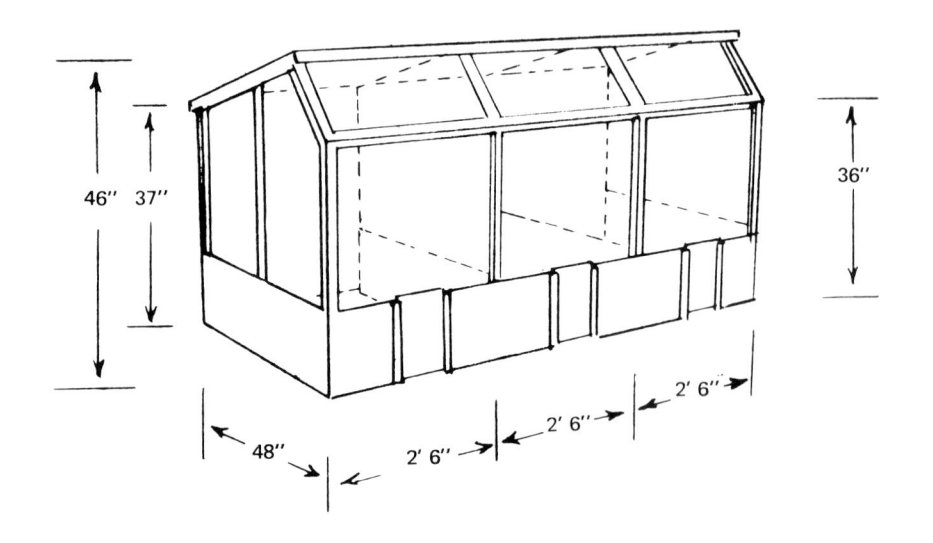

*Design B - Quail Pens*

Some people prefer to see their birds housed at ground level with shrubs growing; this can be achieved by using this type of pen. A small flowering or evergreen shrub can be planted in the soil to the front of the pens; the floor then covered in 2" (50mm) of sand, this will prevent earthworms coming to the surface which are the host to various types of disease. If the pen is decorated with a few logs and some dried grass or leaves, the birds will soon feel at home, and when the breeding season comes around, will make a natural nest, and if required, will attempt to hatch and brood their own chicks. Because the front of these pens is exposed to the elements, it is well to arrange some sort of cover for the food dish.

*Design C - Quail Aviaries*

These were designed as a permanent structure, giving each pair of birds ample room to live as naturally as possible, being suitably planted with shrubs and grasses to resemble their natural habitat. At the end of each aviary there is a house in which the birds have their food and water, being raised off the ground the birds will soon learn to roost in them.

### Housing For Less Hardy Species

For those species which require protection during the winter from frost and cold, a small garden shed divided up internally into a number of pens is usually satisfactory, an external run is also an advantage being connected to the building by a pop hole through which the Quail are able to enter the shed. It is up to the individual preference as to the type of heating to use. A number of people are using small 1Kw blower heaters regulated by a thermostat cutting in when the temperature drops below 50°F in the winter months.

### Catching Birds

People often ask how does one catch the birds when housed in the pens described. The method is very simple; obtain a child's fishing net and attach the net section to a long bamboo. The Quail can be caught and drawn to the front of the cage; being only a small net the birds are not damaged in the process and can be easily handled.

## DESIGN 'C'

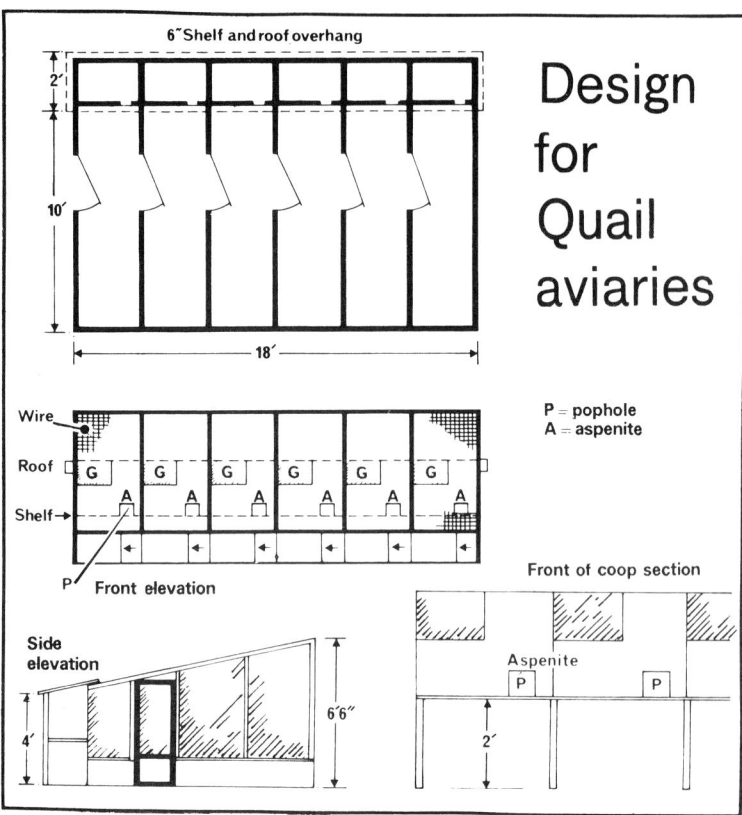

# Design for Quail aviaries

Design of a range of six Quail aviaries constructed by Keith Howman.

Egg Collection
As with catching the birds, collecting eggs laid on the floor of any of the houses can be achieved by using a bamboo with a piece of heavy gauge wire bent into a ring of no more than 1″ (25mm) diameter, attached to one end, this can be slid under the egg, which can then be lifted out.

# CHAPTER 3

## GENERAL MANAGEMENT AND HUSBANDRY

Perhaps the most important aspect of keeping Quail is their management, which means care and detail. Anyone can throw a handful of food into the house once a day and then clear off to work. The birds might well survive for a long time, but if you are keen to breed and raise the rarer species, it is necessary to take a little more care. As with a shepherd who knows each sheep by sight and their individual traits, the Quail breeder should go to the same trouble and check each bird visually each day to see if it is still in good condition; a bird sitting in the corner looking miserable is always the first sign that things ae not right. Regular feeding is always recommended, some breeders prefer to feed daily, rather than giving their birds food hoppers to feed on an ad lib basis. Personally, I have to feed all the adult stock by the ad lib principle for two reasons; one, to save time, and the other, to prevent hungry birds picking at anything they come across, which could well be each other; this is not to say my birds are not checked every day.

To help the person who has not come across sickness in his birds before, listed are the main common ailments likely to be encountered.

### Common Ailments

*Infectious Sinusitus*
Cause: Infection with various micro-organisms such as aspergillosis, staphylococci, psittacosis, or tumour formation within the sinus.
Signs: A discharge from the nostrils, usually of a thick nature.
Treatment: Antibiotics could be useful in certain cases (Tylan), in others, the administration of Potassium iodide (1 teaspoonful of a 1% solution to 2 oz of drinking water daily). Vitamins given on a regular basis will help to strengthen the bird's resistance.

*Bronchitis and Pneumonia*
Cause: Infection as with Sinusitus, or draughts and subsequent chilling.
Signs: Birds labour in breathing, gaping or gasping with squeaking on respiration. Also birds are inclined to keep their wings away from the body. Sinusitus may also be present.
Treatment: Isolate into a hospital pen, at a temperature of 70-75°F, inhalations of Friars Balsam could be of help. Antibiotics may be used with the approval of your Vet.

*Chronic Respiratory Disease*
Cause: Infection with a micro-organism
Signs: Nasal discharge and sniffing, together with a swelling of the face, loss of appetite and depression are noticeable, with a general decline in body weight.
Treatment: Use of antibiotics is the best treatment, (Tylan, Auromycin or Tiamulin), together with increased ventilation in their quarters.

*Enteritis: Inflammation of the Intestine*
Cause: Ingestion of contaminated food or water, unsuitable foods, or specific infectious diseases, also can be associated with the micro-organisms E.Coli in the gut.
Signs: The affected bird shows excessive thirst and a craving for grit. Profuse, greenish diarrhoea. The vent becomes stained and matted with droppings.
Treatment: Place in hospital pen, at a temperature of 70-80°F, with attention paid to diet. Antibiotics may be given (Neomycin or Streptomycin).

*Blackhead*
Cause: A protozoan disease which affects all types of game birds, being transmitted by caecal worms.
Signs: An affected bird shows signs of lowered head and wings, drowsiness, ruffled feathers and a yellowish diarrhoea, although young birds may die without showing signs of the disease.
Treatment: Prevention is the best treatment, transferring the birds to clean ground. Affected birds can be treated with Emtryl,

although most compounded chick crumbs do include a minimal prevention dose of an anti-blackhead drug.

*Coccidiosis*
Cause: A protozoan disease which affects the intestines.
Signs: Affected birds show emaciation, anaemia, green slimy diarrhoea, diminishing appetite and increased thirst, sudden death will occur in a proportion of birds.
Treatment: Sulphadimidine Solution 16%, 10 drops in 1oz. of drinking water for 3 days, repeating the course after an interval of 2 days. Strict attention must be paid to diet and hygiene. Veradin can be used under direction of your Vet.
Terramycin - as a broad spectrum antibiotic
Tylan - for sinusitis.

*Scaly-Leg*
Cause: By mites of the *Cnemidocoptes* species
Signs: Scaliness of the legs, with honeycomb appearance, nodular masses form around the legs.
Treatment: Acriflavine emulsion 1 part to 1000, apply daily for 2 weeks or Gamma B.H.C. 0.02% in soft paraffin.

*Newcastle Disease or Fowl pest*
Cause: A virus disease found primarily in domestic poultry and is notifiable in Great Britain.
Signs: In newly imported birds, sudden death without previous signs may be encountered, possibly difficult breathing, loss of use of legs and backward bending of the head are noticeable.
Treatment: As a notifiable disease, no treatment is allowed, contact your vet immediately.

*Worms*
Worms live in the small intestine of the birds with eggs passed in the droppings. Generally worms cause a stunting of the growth in young stock and adult birds become droopy. Treatment can be in the form of periodic worming medication in the feed or water.

Treatment: Thiabenzole as per instructions, or Mebenvet at the rate of 1 oz. per 7 lbs of food for 3-5 days. To keep your birds in good condition, a dose prior to and after the breeding season is recommended.

### Vet's Advice

Should there be any doubt always consult your vet. In fact, you now have to obtain most of the drugs mentioned from him in the U.K. as they are no longer allowed to be sold on the open market. Therefore, providing your vet agrees every breeder with more than a few pairs should keep a small drug cupboard stocked with the following for emergencies:

| | |
|---|---|
| Mebenvet | - as a wormer |
| Emtryl | - against Blackhead |
| Veradin | - against Coccidiosis |
| Terramycin | - as a broad spectrum antibiotic |
| Tylan | - for Sinusitis |

### Administration of Medicine

Always avoid handling your birds, as when they are off colour they become very stressed, therefore it is always better to administer drugs through their food and water, that is of course, providing they are not too sick to eat or drink.

### Disinfection

Following any infectious disease, all houses and aviaries should be thoroughly disinfected and scrubbed with hot washing soda or Dettol at the rate of 1 in 20 solution. Should you decide to use Izal or Jeyes Fluid, at the rate of 1 in 10 solutions, care should be taken as these fluids have a caustic action and could damage the feet of the birds unless perches etc. are well scrubbed with plain water after the soaking.

For open flights with natural earth or gravel base, the top soil or gravel should be removed from the flight and buried. Lime (1 lb per sq. yard) should be applied and allowed to remain for one week. This should then be dug over and a new layer of soil or gravel placed on top. Birds should not be returned for at least one week after treatment.

# CHAPTER 4

## FEEDING

*Modern Poultry Foods*

### Chick Diet

Today the aviculturist has at his disposal quite a number of foods which have been specially formulated for the poultry industry; these include in addition to the basic cereal ingredients, high quality animal and vegetable proteins, sources of unidentified growth factors, minerals, trace elements and vitamins. Some also have an anti-coccidiostat added in strictly regulated proportions.

Most food compounders make a range of poultry foods graded by size and protein levels. In the first days of life quail chicks should be fed on starter crumbs (28% protein), ground into a fine powder, using a kitchen hand grinder, the size of the granules depending on the size of the chicks in question. Care should be taken to note if the chicks' flight feathers begin to grow in excess of the rest of it's body; if this occurs, the protein level of the crumbs should be reduced to 20% protein, generally called chick crumbs. In the event of not being able to obtain a range of game foods, turkey starter crumbs will do equally well. After 4 weeks the chicks should be weaned on to the lower protein level of 20% and mixed millet added to their diet. In the early days of life, should there be difficulty in making chicks feed, sprinkle powdered crumbs on the backs of the chicks; this will arouse their interest and start them pecking. The crumbs can be fed on a board or in a pan, but it is a good idea to scatter at least a handful of crumbs on the floor of the brooder to encourage the chicks to hunt for their food. This greatly helps overcome boredom and will assist against feather pecking. It should be remembered when giving dry crumbs that there should in fact be a continual supply available so that the chicks can feed as and when they wish, with a constant water supply.

## Adult Diet

In North America they feed a mixture to their quail as follows:-
6 parts wheat
6 parts milo
3 parts oat groats
2 parts buckwheat
8 parts millet
1/10 parts chick grit 1/40 parts coarse salt
25 parts chick crumbs
¼ part rape seed

For all Quail except Chinese Painted and Harlequin, who have -
4 parts finch seed
4 parts starter crumbs
2 parts layers mash
1/10 part fine grit
1/20 part crushed oyster shell
1/20 part mineral grit
1/40 part coarse salt

All birds having a few drops of cod liver oil, plus vitamin powder.

(by courtesy of T.R.Warwick, Blenheim, Canada).

In the U.K., a diet of two parts chick crumbs and one part mixed millet will satisfy your breeding stock through the winter, added limestone grit and vitamin powder starting in January each year, and finishing at completion of the breeding season. Always feed ad lib allowing the birds to take their own requirements, unlike waterfowl, quail will only eat as much as they need. Feed green food when available at least once a week, but most important to see that it is fed dry, not after a rain storm, or dew in the morning, wet greens can upset the bird's digestion.

## Live Food

With some of the more difficult chicks to rear, such as Mountain Quail, the addition of live food is an advantage. If you cut some stinging nettles and shake them over a large piece of paper, usually many small insects will fall out, and if these are fed on the same dish as the starter crumbs, the chicks will chase around and peck at the insects, thus consuming some of the crumbs, also there are special insect traps with a light inside which can be put out at night to attract insects.

Maggots are used on occasions, but not recommended, as they can carry botulism and therefore must be well cleansed in bran or sawdust for at least three to four days. In fact, their bodies must not show any colour inside before feeding them to the chicks. They are normally obtained from a fishing shop and sold by the ounce. There are various types; the best being called pinkies, a small pink coloured maggot ideal because of its size. Mealworms are both the cleanest and most practical insect to feed, they only require a few inches of bran to be maintained. Choose a container such as an aquarium to house them, place layers of newspaper or sacking on top of the bran. The mealworms like getting between the layers and can be easily collected. The reproductive cycle of a mealworm is fairly slow and that is the reason why they are so expensive to buy. They can be obtained from either your pet shop, or via one of the weekly newspapers dealing with birds.

### Grit

It plays a major part of a bird's digestive system, being consumed and deposited in their gizzard; this grinds the food into a paste, allowing the food to be digested. There are two forms of grit, each having a different purpose, to assist digestion is granite or flint, which are very small stones broken in pieces, and the other form of grit is limestone or oyster shell, which is soluble and is intended for laying birds and should be provided during the laying season to replace the calcium that goes into making the egg shells.

### Food Additives

To bring breeding stock into condition and for healthy birds throughout the year, a vitamin-mineral supplement is essential, being sprinkled on to the food each day at the rate of one teaspoonful per 8 birds. There are a number of makes on the market, all of which have most of the following ingredients :-

## Minerals:

| | |
|---|---|
| Calcium and Phosphorus | for strong, sturdy bones |
| Iodine | for efficient thyroid function |
| Sodium Chloride E.P. | - for proper acid-base balance |
| Iron and Copper | - for formation of haemoglobin - the oxygen carrier |
| Cobalt | - to prevent anaemia and poor growth in some species |
| Magnesium | - for proper functioning of the neuro-muscular system |
| Manganese | - for bone formation growth and reproduction |

## Vitamins:

| | |
|---|---|
| Vitamin A | - for resistance to disease and formation of bones |
| Vitamin B1 (Thiamine Mononitrate SUP) | - for healthy nervous system appetite and digestion |
| Vitamin B2 (Riboflavin BP) | - for optimal growth and function of all body cells |
| Vitamin B6 (Pyridoxine Hydrochloride B.P.) | - for metabolism of proteins |
| Vitamin B12 (Cyanocobalamin EP) | - to promote growth and improve hatchability of eggs |
| Calcium Pantothenate U.S.P | - for good feather development growth and appetite |
| Folic Acid B.P. | - essential to growth, reproduction and normal feathering |
| Choline chloride | - to help in metabolism of dietary fats |
| Vitamin.E | - for normal reproduction and muscle development |
| Menadione U.S.N.F. | - for production of prothrombin, the anti-haemorrhagic in the blood |

*The following proprietary brands available:-*

Vionate - E.R.Squibb and Sons Ltd., Animal Health Divn., Regal House, Twickenham, Middx.

P.Y.M. - Phillips Yeast Products Ltd., Park Royal Rd., London NW10 7JX

## CHAPTER 5

### Quail Species

There has been very little written giving a complete list of Quail found throughout the world; with this in mind a comprehensive list has been prepared from a check-list of the Birds of the World by E.S.Gruson, against which basic information has been collected to give the aviculturist the necessary data for identification of species, or sub-species, habitat, and distribution in the world, together with avicultural notes for those quail known to be kept in captivity.

### Species for the beginner

As with Pheasants, there are certain species which have been kept in captivity for many years, and therefore became accustomed to a domestic environment. The Japanese Quail *Coturnix japonica* and the Chinese Painted Quail *E. chinensis* are most suitable for the first-time keeper of quail. They can then progress to the Californian Quail *Callipepla californica* and the Bobwhite Quail *Colinus virginianus*. Once these have been mastered, progress can then be made in keeping and breeding the more difficult species. In the avicultural notes against each species an indication has been given regarding its suitability for the beginner.

### Purchase of Stock

All too often birds are advertised for sale as a true pair, with complete disregard to the fact that they may be brother and sister, and if this practice continues for many generations, one begins to see a species decline genetically, so that lack of fertility, or deformed young could well result. Therefore, it is essential that unrelated birds are obtained. This can be done in three ways:

a) buy the cock and hen from different sources - this always sounds a lot easier than in practice. Most breeders are reluctant to sell just a hen bird, leaving a surplus of cocks at the end of the season. Therefore always buy the hen bird first and then a cock bird.
b) Buy from a dealer of repute, they usually have a through-put of a large number of birds each season, thereby being able to select an unrelated pair.
c) The fail-safe method is to buy two pairs of the same species from different sources, then swap the cock birds over. The surplus pair can then be sold as unrelated, or kept as an insurance.

Always buy your stock from a successful breeder, who has consistently good results, as he is likely to have good breeding birds.

Quail are rarely sold as adult stock, and care should be taken when introducing an older bird with younger stock. This can result in the younger bird being beaten up, or even killed. Therefore, young birds should be purchased.

By the age of 12-14 weeks most quail should show adult feathering and can easily be identified, male from female, although it is always better to buy birds which are in full plumage and hatched early in the season. Always try and obtain good looking quail. Poor birds do from time to time prove to be good breeders, but it is always best to attempt to begin with perfect birds.

Young birds too should always be purchased fully feathered and not minus tail or back feathers, due to feather pecking. Birds denuded of feathers cannot be expected to survive out-door conditions in the way a normal feathered bird can - so if you have the chance to see the birds before accepting delivery, avoid those which have been feather-pecked.

*Phasianidae* - Quails

| | |
|---|---|
| 1. Bearded Tree Quail | °*Dendrortyx barbatus* |
| 2. Longtailed Tree Quail | °*Dendrortyx macroura* |
| 3. Buffycrowned Tree Quail | °*Dendrortyx leucophrys* |

| | | |
|---|---|---|
| 4. | Mountain Quail | °*Oreortyx picta* |
| 5. | Scaled Quail | °*Callipepla squamata* |
| 6. | California Quail | °*Callipepla californica* |
| 7. | Gambel's Quail | °*Callipepla gambelii* |
| 8. | Elegant Quail | °*Callipepla douglasii* |
| 9. | Banded Quail | °*Philortyx fasciatus* |
| 10. | Bobwhite Quail | °*Colinus virginianus* |
| 11. | Blackthroated Bobwhite Quail | *Colinus nigrogularis* |
| 12. | Crested Bobwhite Quail | °*Colinus cristatus* |
| 13. | Marbled Quail | *Odontophorus gujanensis* |
| 14. | Spotwinged Wood Quail | *Odontophorus capueira* |
| 15. | Rufousfronted Wood Quail | *Odontophorus erythrops* |
| 16. | Blackfronted Wood Quail | *Odontophorus atrifrons* |
| 17. | Darkbacked Wood Quail | *Odontophorus melanonotus* |
| 18. | Chestnut Wood Quail | *Odontophorus hyperythrus* |
| 19. | Rufousbreasted Wood Quail | *Odontophorus speciosus* |
| 20. | Gorgeted Wood Quail | *Odontophorus strophium* |
| 21. | Tacaruna Wood Quail | *Odontophorus dialencos* |
| 22. | Venezuelan Wood Quail | *Odontophorus columbianus* |
| 23. | Whitethroated Wood Quail | *Odontophorus leucolaemus* |
| 24. | Stripefaced Wood Quail | *Odontophorus balliviani* |
| 25. | Starred Wood Quail | *Odontophorus stellatus* |
| 26. | Spotted Wood Quail | *Odontophorus guttatus* |
| 27. | Singing Quail | *Dactylortyx thoracicus* |
| 28. | Mearns Quail | ° *Cyntonyx montizumae* |
| 29. | Ocellated Quail | *Cyntonyx ocellatus* |
| 30. | Tawnyfaced Quail | *Rhynchortyx cinctus* |
| 31. | Eurasian Quail | °*Coturnix coturnix* |
| 32. | Japanese Quail | °*Coturnix japonica* |
| 33. | Rain Quail | °*Coturnix coromandelica* |
| 34. | Harlequin Quail | °*Coturnix delegorouei* |
| 35. | Chinese Painted Quail | ° *Excalfactoria chinensis* |
| 36. | Pectoral Quail | °*Coturnix pectoralis* |
| 37. | New Zealand Quail | *Coturnix novazelandiae* |
| 38. | Brown Quail | °*Coturnix (Synoicus) ysilophorus* |
| 39. | Snow Mountain Quail | *Anurophasis monorthonyx* |
| 40. | Indian Mountain Quail | *Ophrysia superciliosa* |

41. Jungle Bush Quail     °*Perdicula asiatica*
42. Rock Bush Quail     °*Perdicula argoondah*
43. Painted Bush Quail     °*Perdicula erythrorhyncha*
44. Manipur Bush Quail     *Perdicula manipurensis*

° 22 recorded species held in captivity per the W.P.A. Census 1978. However, there may be other species not currently recorded.

**Ref.** Checklist of the *Birds of the World* - **E.S. Gruson. 1976.**

---

## Bearded Tree Quail     *Dendrortyx barbatus*
bearded wood partridge     (Gould 1846)

Subspecies:
None described

### Habitat
Mountain forests

### Description
Adults. 9"-13" (230-255mm) in length. (Males 5mm longer on average). Sexes alike. Grey throat, and chest; a buffy brown crown and cinnamon brown breast and abdomen; upper back reddish brown edged with grey, while lower back is mottled with olive brown, black and tawny. Bill, legs, feet and bare skin around the eyes are all red.

### Distribution
State of Vera Cruz Mexico, Northward to Eastern San Luis Potori and Eastern Hidalgo.

**Reference:** *Grouse and Quails of North America.* P.A. Johnsgard.

5:1

**Bobwhite Quail (Eastern) ♀**
*Colinus virginianus*

**Bobwhite Quail ♂**
*Colinus virginianus*

**Chestnut Bellied Scaled Quail ♀ ♂**
*Callipepla squamata*

**Chestnut Bellied Scaled Quail ♂**
*Callipepla squamata*

**Montezuma Quail (Mearns)** ♂
*Cyntonyx montezumae*

**Rain Quail** ♂
*Coturnix coromandelica*

**Montezuma Quail (Mearns)** ♂
*Cyntonyx montezumae*

**Montezuma Quail (Mearns)** ♀
*Cyntonyx montezumae*

## Long-tailed Tree Quail

*Dendrortyx macroura*
(Jardine & Selby 1828)

long-tailed partridge
long-tailed wood partridge

Subspecies:
*D.m.macroura* - eastern long-tailed tree quail
*D.m.griseipectus* - grey-breasted tree quail
*D.m.diversus* - jalisco long-tailed tree quail
*D.m.striatus* - guenero long-tailed tree quail
*D.m.oaxacae* - Oaxacae long-tailed tree quail
*D.m.inesparatus* - (Phillips described 1966 not in Mexican check list)

### Habitat
Dense underbrush of mountain slopes

### Description
Adults 12¼"-13½" (305-380mm) in length. Sexes alike. Black throat and forehead, blackish feathers around the ears; a bushy brown crest, and the upper back and chest are reddish brown, edged with grey, lower back is mottled with brown, black and tawny, the breast is grey, streaked with reddish brown, grading to olive on the sides and abdomen. Bill, legs, feet, bare skin around eyes are all red. This is the largest and heaviest of North American Quail, and with the other two species (bearded and buffy-crowned quail) which have extremely long tails.

### Distribution
Highlands of Mexico from Michoacan and Vera Cruz, South to Oaxaca.

Reference: *Grouse and Quails of North America* - P.A.Johnsgard

# Buffy-crowned Tree Quail

Buffy-fronted wood partridge

*Dendrortyx leucophrys*
(Gould 1844)

Subspecies:
*D.l.leucophrys* (Gould 1844)   Guatemala
El Salvador
Honduras
Nicaragua
*D.l.hypospodius* (Salvin 1896) Costa Rica

**Natural Habitat**
Mountain forest, secondary forest, grassy or bushy areas at elevations 1,000m-2,900m.

**Description**
Adults 12½"-13½" (318-356mm) in length. Sexes similar. Forepart of crown and throat pale buff or whitish; molar region and auriculars blackish, finely streaked paler, rear crown, hind neck and sides of neck chestnut, the two last streaked or spotted white; mantle, scapulars, and back bluish grey, boldly striped chestnut, outer webs of flight feathers reddish brown, rump, upper tail coverts and tail dusky or olive brown, the outer retrices often reddish, sometimes narrowly barred; underparts mainly bluish grey, brownish on flanks, the lower throat, foreneck and breast striped chestnut or black, under tail coverts sooty. Eyes yellowish or grey olive, bare skin of orbital region and feet orange red; bill black, the lower mandible orange below.

**Distribution**
Extreme Southern Mexico and Guatemala, South to Costa Rica

**Reference:***Manual of Neotropical Birds* - E.R.Blake.

## Mountain Quail

*Oreortyx pictus*
(Douglas 1872)

Plumed Quail
Mountain Quail
Painted Quail

Subspecies:
*O.p.pictus* - Sierra Mountain Quail
*O.p.palmeci* - Coast Mountain Quail
*O.p.conifis* - San Pedro Mountain Quail
*O.p.eremophila* - Desert Mountain Quail
*O.p.russelli* - Pallid Mountain Quail

### Natural Habitat
Dense bush, coniferous forest, edges of mountain, meadows and sometimes high crests. During the breeding season found between 1,500 feet and 10,000 feet.

### Description
Adults 9½"-11½" (267-292mm) in length. Sexes similar, having straight narrow blackish crest comprising of two feathers, throat is chestnut, edged with black, a white line separates the slate-grey chest, neck and head, olive-grey on the back, wings and tail, flanks are dark brown with vertically placed black and white lines.

### Distribution
Western United States from Southern Washington and South-Western Idaho, East to Nevada and South to Baja California, introduced to West Washington and West British Columbia - Vancouver Island.

### Avicultural Notes
| | |
|---|---|
| Recommended aviary size | 48"(1.25m) x 48"(1.25m) |
| Number in captivity | 172 (WPA Census 1978) |
| Egg clutch size | 6-15 eggs |
| Egg colour | pale buff to cream |
| Incubation period | 24-25 days |

5:4

| | |
|---|---|
| Noise level | moderate to loud |
| Habits | ground dwelling |
| Food | 20% protein chick crumbs, mixed millet, occasional live food. |
| Novice selection | difficult |
| Special Note | chicks to be reared apart from other species to prevent beak and toe pecking |

## Scaled Quail

Scaled Partridge
Blue-racer Quail
Blue Quail
Cottontop Quail
Mexican Quail
Top-knot Quail

*Callipepla squamata*
(Vigors 1830)

Subspecies:

*C.s.squamata*     - Mexican scaled
*C.s.pallida*     - Arizona scaled
*C.s.cantanogasruis* - Chestnut bellied

### Natural Habitat

Desert grasslands, thorn scrub and juniper savannah. Chestnut bellied found in open prickly-pear cactus flats.

### Description

Adults 9½"-12¼" (255-305mm) in length. Blue-grey colour, and marked on the back, breast and abdomen with blackish scale markings, crest bushy, males whitish and females buff, head grey-brown, the lower back, wings and tail are brown-grey changing to grey, flanks grey to brown with light shaft markings. Males *(Cantanogasruis)* have chestnut colour similar to the male California Quail. Females can be distinguished from the adult males by the dark shaft-streaks on side of face and throat.

### Distribution

South Arizona, Northern Mexico, Eastern Colorado and Southern Kansas, South to Southern Mexico. Central Washington and Eastern Nevada.

### Avicultural Notes

Recommended aviary size    48"(1.25m) x 48"(1.25m)
Number in captivity    202 (WPA Census 1978)
Egg clutch size    5-22 eggs

| | |
|---|---|
| Egg colour | pale buff to cream - slight spotting |
| Incubation period | 23 days |
| Noise level | reasonable |
| Habits | ground dwelling, roosts off ground if allowed |
| Food | 20% protein crumbs, white millet, live food occasionally, chickweed in breeding season |
| Novice selection | not suitable |

# California Quail

*Callipepla californica*
(Shaw 1798)

Crested Quail
Catalina Quail
Top-knot Quail
Valley Quail

Subspecies:
| | | |
|---|---|---|
| *C.californica* | - | Valley californica quail |
| *C.catalina* | - | Catalina Is. californica quail |
| *C.plumbea* | - | San Quentin californica quail |
| *C.achrustera* | - | San Lucas californica quail |
| *C.canfieldae* | - | Inyo californica quail |
| *C.orecta* | - | Great Basin californica quail |
| *C.decoloratus* | - | Baja californica quail |
| *C.crunnescens* | - | Coastal californica quail |

## Natural Habitat
Valleys and rain shadow areas, dominated by grasslands or semi-desert sage bush scrub, chaparal vegetation and scrubby tropical forest.

## Description
Adults 9½"-10½" (240-280mm) in length. Sexes different. Males have black throat and chestnut belly, chocolate-brown behind plume, forward tilting blackish crests which are enlarged into a tear-drop shape. Both sexes have clear blue-grey to grey chest, becoming buff towards abdomen and have darker scaly markings similar to Scaled Quail. Female has smaller comma-type crest.

## Distribution
Southern Oregon and Western Nevada, South to the tip of Baja California.

## Avicultural Notes
Recommended aviary size 48"(1.25m) x 48"(1.25m)

| | |
|---|---|
| Number in captivity | 744 (WPA Census 1978) |
| Egg clutch size | 10-14 eggs |
| Egg colour | pale buff to cream with moderate spotting |
| Incubation period | 22-23 days |
| Noise level | reasonable call |
| Habits | will perch given an opportunity |
| Food | 20% protein, chick crumbs and white millet |
| Novice selection | ideal |
| Special Note | chicks can be difficult to rear at an early age. |

## Gambel's Quail  *Callipepla gambelii*
(Gambel 1843)

Desert Quail
Arizona Quail

Subspecies:
| | |
|---|---|
| *C.p.gambelii* | - South Western Gambel's Quail |
| *C.p.fulipectus* | - Fulvous-breasted Gambel's Quail |
| *C.p.pembertoni* | - Tiburon Istan Gambel's Quail |
| *C.p.sama* | - Colorado Gambel's Quail |
| *C.p.ignoscens* | - Texas Gambel's Quail |
| *C.p.stephensi* | - Not verified |
| *C.p.friedmann* | - Sinaloa Gambel's Quail |

**Natural Habitat**
Desert valleys, upland desert and river basins.

**Description**
Adults 9½"-10½" (240-280mm) in length. Black teardrop crest forward tilting, lacks scaly pattern as with Californian, only on the back of neck of the male is some scaly pattern to be found, males have a black forehead and reddish-brown crown, both sexes have red-brown flanks, as opposed to brown with Californian, otherwise the birds are grey-brown to brown on the tail and upper parts, buffy underparts which may be streaked with brown on the female, males have a black area on the abdomen, together with the characteristic black throat pattern.

**Distribution**
West Colorado, South to North-Eastern Baja California, Central Sonara, North-Western Chihuahua and Western Texas to Southern Nevada, and South Utah.

**Avicultural Notes**
| | |
|---|---|
| Recommended size of aviary | 48"(1.25m) x 48"(1.25m) |
| Number in captivity | 631 (WPA Census 1978) |
| Egg clutch size | 6-19 eggs |

| | |
|---|---|
| Egg colour | pale buff to white with moderate spotting |
| Incubation period | 22 days |
| Noise level | reasonable |
| Habits | ground dwelling, but will roost off ground |
| Food | 20% protein crumbs, white millet |
| Novice selection | ideal - easy to rear. |

## Elegant Quail          *Callipepla douglasii*
(Vigors 1829)

Benson Quail
Crested Quail
Douglas Quail
Yaqui Quail

Subspecies:
*C.d.douglasii*
*C.d.benson*
*C.d.teres*
*C.d.impedita*
*C.d.languens*

### Natural Habitat
Tropical deciduous forest, thorn forest foothills and scrub thickets of river valleys.

### Description
Adults 8"-9½" (229-255mm) in length. Females - head colour mostly brown, males grey streaked or spotted with black, and with a straight, pointed crest of graduated feathers, orange buff in males, mottled brown in females, upper parts of back, wings and tail are uniform grey in males.

### Distribution
South West Jalisco to South-Eastern Guaneio, Mexico.

### Avicultural Notes

| | |
|---|---|
| Recommended aviary size | 48"(1.25m) x 48"(1.25m) |
| Number in captivity | 13 (WPA Census 1978) |
| Egg clutch size | 8-12 eggs |
| Egg colour | white |
| Incubation period | 22 days |
| Noise level | moderate |
| Habits | ground dwelling |
| Food | 20% protein crumbs, mixed millets, live food |
| Novice selection | not suitable |
| Special note | may not lay until second year in captivity. Protect from frost. |

## Barred or Banded Quail
*Philortyx fasciatus*
(Gould 1844)

Subspecies:
Not described

### Natural Habitat
Dense weed patches, farmland, open bushy slopes

### Description
Adults. 7¾"-8½" (204-216mm) in length. The sexes are almost identical in appearance. This small quail has a brown to greyish white head with semi-straight crest of several feathers which are barred with black and brown. The body is generally greyish-brown to grey with flanks ad breast barred vertically with brownish black and white. Females are generally browner in head and neck, the crests are also smaller.

### Distribution
South and Central Mexico, Pacific slope from Jalisco to Guenero, inland through Michoacan to Puebla.

### Avicultural notes

| | |
|---|---|
| Recommended aviary size | 48"(1.25m) x 48"(1.25m) |
| Number in captivity | 2 (WPA Census 1978). |
| Egg clutch size | 14-16 eggs. |
| Egg colour | white. |
| Incubation period | 22-23 days. |
| Noise level | quiet, except for a squeal when flushed. |
| Habits | will roost off the ground. |
| Food | high protein crumbs and mixed millet. |
| Novice selection | not suitable. |
| Special note | rare. |

# Bobwhite Quail    *Colinus virginianus*
(Linnaeus 1758)

American Coton
Partridge Quail

Subspecies: (21 known)

| | |
|---|---|
| *C.v.virginianus* | - Eastern Bobwhite |
| *C.v.marilandicus* (Linnaeus) | - New England Bobwhite |
| *C.v.mexicanus* (Linnaeus) | - Interior Bobwhite |
| *C.v.floridanus* (Cones) | - Florida Bobwhite |
| *C.v.texanus* (Lawrence) | - Texas Bobwhite |
| *C.v.taylori* (Lincoln) | - Plains Bobwhite |
| *C.v.ridgewayi* (Brewster) | - Masked Bobwhite |
| *C.v.cubanensis* (Gray) | - Cuban Bobwhite |
| *C.v.maculatus* (Nelson) | - Spotted-bellied Bobwhite |
| *C.v.aridus* (Aldrich) | - Jaumave Bobwhite |
| *C.v.graysoni* (Lawrence) | - Grayson Bobwhite |
| *C.v.nigripectus* (Nelson) | - Puebla Bobwhite |
| *C.v.pectoralis* (Gould) | - Black-breasted Bobwhite |
| *C.v.godmani* (Nelson) | - Godman Bobwhite |
| *C.v.minor* (Nelson) | - Least Bobwhite |
| *C.v.insignis* (Nelson) | - Guatemalan Bobwhite |
| *C.v.coyolcos* (Muller) | - Coyolcos Bobwhite |
| *C.v.salvini* (Nelson) | - Salvini Bobwhite |
| *C.v.thayeri* (Bangs & Peters) | - Thayer Bobwhite |
| *C.v.atriceps* (Ogilvie-Grant) | - Blackheaded Bobwhite |
| *C.v.nelsoni* (Bnodkorb) | - Nelson Bobwhite |

Reference: *Grouse and Quails of N.America*  P.A.Johnsgard

## Habitat
Wooded or bushy river valleys to mixed grass prairies, tree thickets adjacent to pasture lands.

## Description
Adults 9.5"-10.6"(240-272mm) in length. Sexes different. Males vary greatly in colouration in different parts of the species range.

## DISTRIBUTION OF THE BOBWHITE QUAIL

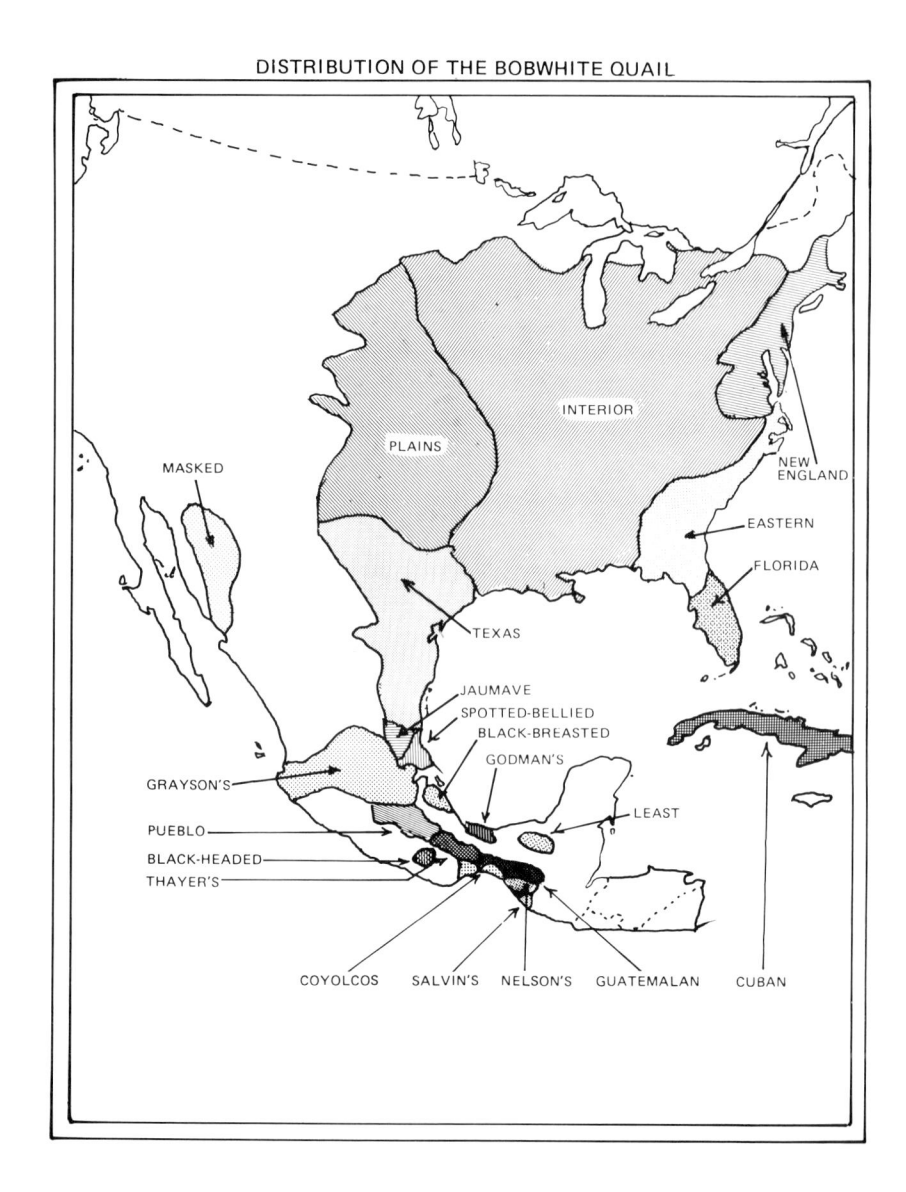

Males of most races, however, have a white eye stripe that extends from the bill through the eye back to the base of the neck, with brown or brownish black colouration above. The ear region is blackish to hazel brown in males, and this feathering extends backwards below the white eye-stripe and expands under the throat to form a blackish chest collar under the white chin and throat of most races. Certain subspecies, the chin and throat are black with the lower chest being blackish brown. In the northern subspecies, the breast and abdomen are irregularly barred with black and white. In Southern Mexico the subspecies have a generally darker underpart and do not have white markings. Females of all subspecies have buff chins, upper throats, and eye stripes, with buffy tones replacing the white underpart colour of the male; they also lack black collars and in general are more heavily marked with brown and buff barring both above and below.

### Distribution

See attached map covering the 21 known subspecies.

### Avicultural notes

| | |
|---|---|
| Recommended aviary size | 48"(1.25m) x 48"(1.25m) |
| Number in captivity | 2,585 (WPA Census 1978) |
| Egg clutch size | 7-28 eggs |
| Egg colour | white |
| Incubation period | 22-23 days |
| Noise level | reasonable |
| Habits | Prone to fight if males left together |
| Food | chick crumbs, millets, little green food |
| Novice selection | ideal for beginners having graduated from Coturnix |
| Special note | Chicks will feather and toe peck if too crowded, inclined to fight if housed with other species. |
| | As there are many subspecies available it is most important they are not crossed, thus retaining a true race. |

## Black-throated Bobwhite Quail — *Colinus nigrogularis* (Gould 1843)

Subspecies:
*C.n.nigrogularis* (Gould 1843)   Belize, N.Guatemala
*C.n.segoviensis* (Ridgeway 1888) Honduras, N.Nicaragua

**Natural Habitat**
Forest clearing, tropical zone in pine savannahs, overgrown fields and plantations.

**Description**
Adults 7½"-8½" (190-215mm) in length. Male - throat and molar region black bordered with white; a broad black eyestripe; forehead and sides of pileum white, the crown mainly black; behind neck, mantle and sides of body rufous, heavily spotted with white; uppersurfaces of body, wings and tail mottled and barred with grey and brown; scapulars and tertials spotted and barred with black and rufous, feathers of the breast and abdomen white with broad black margins, appearing boldly scalloped, lower belly and undertail coverts uniformly cinnamon. Eyes brown, bill black, feet brown to grey blue. Female - similar to male, except behind neck and mantle black with pale spotting, throat tawny buff, below white; more or less heavily barred and streaked with black and rufous brown.

**Distribution**
Yucatan peninsula, South to Honduras and Nicaragua

**Indian Mountain Quail** ♀ ♂
*Ophrysia superciliosa*

**Mountain Quail**
*Oreortyx picta*

**Mountain Quail**
*Oreortyx picta*

**Harlequin Quail** ♂
*Coturnix delegorouei*

**Harlequin Quail** ♀
*Coturnix delegorouei*

**Jungle Bush Quail** ♂
*Perdicula asiatica*

**Jungle Bush Quail** ♂ ♀
*Perdicula asiatica*

# Crested Bobwhite Quail *Colinus cristatus* (Linnaeus 1766)

Subspecies:
| | |
|---|---|
| *C.c.marise* (Wetmore 1962) | - Panama |
| *C.C.panamensis* (Dicky & Van Rossen 1930) | - N. Panama |
| *C.c.decoratus* (Todd 1917) | - Colombia |
| *C.c.littoralis* (Todd 1917) | - N. Colombia |
| *C.c.cristatus* (Linnaeus 1766) | - N.E. Colombia |
| *C.c.badius* (Conover 1938) | - Tropical Colombia |
| *C.c.leucotis* (Gould 1844) | - Tropical Colombia |
| *C.c.bogotensis* (Dugand 1943) | - Temperate Colombia |
| *C.c.parvicristatus* (Gould 1843) | - S.W. Venezuela |
| *C.c.continentis* (Cory 1913) | - N.W. Venezuela |
| *C.c.horvathi* (Madarasy 1904) | - N.W. Venezuela |
| *C.c.carnesi* (Gilliard 1940) | - N.E. Venezuela |
| *C.c.macquerysi* (Hartest 1894) | - N.E. Venezuela |
| *C.c.sornini* (Temminck 1815) | - N. Venezuela, N. Brazil |

## Natural Habitat

Tropical to temperate zone in grassy savannahs, thickets and forest edge.

## Description

Adult 7"-8½" (178-216mm) in length. Sexes alike. Male - forehead (or entire crown) and long feathers of crown white or pale buff, the crest feathers alone sometimes dark; hindneck and sides spotted black and white; throat white, buff tawny, or cinnamon, sometimes spotted black, or with a black lateral border; auriculars white or buff, bordered above and below by a black or rufous stripe; upperparts finely mottled grey, brown and black; scapulars and tertials with trimmed black spots, the feathers often edged whitish or buff; below spotted and strongly patterned white, buff, cinnamon, and black, eyes brown, bill black, feet blue grey. Female similar, but pileum mainly brown or buff, speckled or finely streaked black.

**Reference:** *Manual of Neotropical Birds* - E.R. Blake.

## Distribution
Panama and North South America, Aruba, Caracas, Margarita Island, introduced on Mustique Island, Grenadines and St. Thomas, Virgin Islands.

## Avicultural notes

| | |
|---|---|
| Recommended aviary size | 48"(1.25m) x 48"(1.25m) |
| Number in captivity | Captive stock would appear to have died out per Warwick 1980 |
| Egg clutch size | 6-20 eggs |
| Egg colour | pink colour spotted egg |
| Incubation period | 22-23 days |
| Noise level | reasonable |
| Habits | extremely wild species |
| Food | mixed millets, wheat, milo, greenfood, 20% protein chick crumbs |
| Novice selection | not suitable, very rare |
| Special note | species became very inbred. Vito Bucco of U.S.A. maintained stock for a number of years. |
| | T. Warwick, Ontario, Canada gained first breeding in 1978 for Canada. |
| | Will not survive outside with extremes of weather, frost or heavy rain |

## Marbled Wood Quail

*Odontophorus gujanensis*
(Gmelin 1789)

Subspecies:
| | |
|---|---|
| *O.g.castigatus* (Bange 1901) | - Costa Rica, Panama |
| *O.g.marmoratus* (Gould 1844) | - Panama, Columbia, Venezuela |
| *O.g.medius* (Chapman 1929) | - Venezuela, Brazil |
| *O.g.gujanensis* (Gmelin 1789) | - Venezuela, Guianas, Brazil |
| *O.g.buckleyi* (Chubb 1919) | - Columbia, Eucador |
| *O.g.pachyrhynchus* (Tschudi 1844) | - Peru |
| *O.g.regularis* (Blake 1959) | - Peru |
| *O.g.simonsi* (Chubb 1919) | - Bolivia |

### Natural Habitat
Tropical and lower sub-tropical forest and secondary growth

### Description
Adult 9½"-11½" (240-290mm) in length. Sexes similar. Plumage variable, crown and occipital crest reddish brown, or finely barred; sides of head dull chestnut rufous or grey, extending over entire throat, behind neck and mantle brown or grey, finely barred with black, wing coverts and scapulars brown or grey barred and spotted with buff and black, lower back, rump, and upper tail coverts olive or tawny; underside of body grey, often narrowly barred with black and white. Eye hazel or brown, naked skin around the eye vermilion or orange, Bill blue black, legs blue grey.

### Distribution
Panama, S.W.Costa Rica, Northern South America, East of the Andes, South to Eastern Bolivia, Central and North-Eastern Brazil.

Reference: *Manual of Neotropical Birds* - E.R.Blake

## Spot-winged Wood Quail    *Odontophorus capueira*
(Spix 1825)

Subspecies:
*O.c.plumbeicollis* - N.E.Brazil
*O.c.capseirra* - E.Brazil, E.Paraguay, N.Argentina

**Natural Habitat**
Lowland forest

**Description**
Adults 9½"-11½" (265-290mm) in length. Sexes similar. Upper parts similar to *O.gujanensis* (marbled wood quail), but crown and crest reddish brown or deep chestnut, forehead and prominent superciliary stripe paler, more rufous or tawny, mantle brown, less grey and usually with fine pale shaft streaks; flight feathers black, the outer webs spotted white; molar regions, sides of neck, and underparts uniform dark grey, or breast and rear parts somewhat paler and tinged with buff. Eyes brown, with eyelid red, bill black, feet grey black.

**Distribution**
Eastern Brazil, South to Eastern Paraguay and extreme North-Eastern Argentina

**Reference:** *Manual of Neotropical Birds* - E.R.Blake

## Rufous-fronted Wood Quail  *Odontophorus erythrops*
(Gould 1859)

Subspecies:
*O.e.verecundus* (Peters 1929) - Honduras
*O.e.melanotis* (Salvin 1865) - Nicaragua, Costa Rica
*O.e.parambal* (Rothschild 1897) - Colombia, Eucador
*O.e.erythrops* (Gould 1859) - Ecuador

### Natural Habitat
Heavy forest, tropical and lower sub-tropical zones

### Description
Adults 8"-11" (230-280mm) in length. Sexes similar. Colour pattern of head and throat strikingly varied, forehead of crown and sides of head either chestnut rufous like breast, the back of crown and crest dull black, or entire pileum dusky chestnut, throat and sides of foreneck extensively black, sometimes with a conspicuous white gular band, or sides of head fuscous, shading to brownish black on the throat; upperparts mainly sooty black or deep olive; minutely vermiculated with cinnamon; scapulars and back sometimes spotted black; flight feathers fuscous, the outer webs finely barred and vermiculated with cinnamon; breast and sides chestnut rufous; flanks and under-tail coverts cinnamon buff, lightly barred with black, eyes deep red brown in males, coffee brown in females, bare skin around eye purple in males, blue/black in females. Bill black, feet blue/black.

### Distribution
Carribean slope of Central America, from Honduras, Southward, Western Colombia, East to the lower Canca Valley and Southward in Western Eucador to Loja.

**Reference:** *Manual of Neotropical Birds* - E.R.Blake.

# Black-fronted Quail *Odontophorus atrifrous*
(Allen 1900)

Subspecies:
*O.a.atrifrous* (Allen 1900) - Columbia
*O.a.variegatus* (Todd 1919) - Colombia (E.Andes)
*O.a.novai* (Aveleda & Pons) - N.W.Venezuela

## Natural Habitat
Forest, upper tropical and subtropical zones

## Description
Adults 9¾"-10½" (250-270mm) in length. Sexes alike. Male - forehead, (or foreparts of crown); sides of head and throat black; occipital crest (or entire crown) chestnut brown; mantle and upper back grey, finely vermiculated with black; lower back and rump brown, often spotted with black; wings mottled and barred cinnamon and black; scapulars and inner flight feathers with black subterminal spots or bars and white streaks, below mainly olive brown or extensively ochraceous rufous, streaked or spotted white or black. Eyes brown, bill black, feet dusky brown. Female - similar, but medium underparts extensively rufescent.

## Distribution
Santa Marta mountains and Northern end of Eastern Andes, Colombia, North-Western Venezuela.

**Reference:** *Manual of Neotropical Birds* - E.R.Blake

# Dark-backed Wood Quail  *Odontophorus melanotus*
(Gould 1860)

Subspecies:
None known

## Natural Habitat
Lower subtropical zone

## Description
Adults 9½"-10½" (240-270mm) in length. Sexes similar. Sides of head and entire uppersurface deep brownish black, very finely vermiculated with chestnut; flight feathers fuscous, without spots or bars; throat and breast extensively reddish chestnut, palest anteriorly; rear half underparts similar to back, but paler with more brown, eyes brown, bill black, feet and bare skin around eyes brownish black.

## Distribution
North-western Ecuador

**Reference:** *Manual of Neotropical Birds* - E.R.Blake

## Chestnut Wood Quail

*Odontophorus hypnythus*
(Gould 1858)

Subspecies:
None known

**Habitat**
Humid forest in sub-tropical zone.

**Description**
Adults 9¾"-11½" (250-285mm) in length. Sexes different. Male - ear coverts and feathers around the eyes white; pileum dingy chestnut, brightening to rufous chestnut on the sides of head, throat and foreneck; the breast and rear underparts usually paler more orange rufous, upper surfaces of body and wings mainly brown, finely vermiculated with black, the rear of the neck sometimes streaked grey; wing coverts minutely spotted and secondaries finely barred with buff; scapulars boldly spotted black, eyes brown, feet grey. Female - similar, but breast and rear underparts dark grey.

**Distribution**
The Andes of Colombia

**Reference:** *Manual of Neotropical Birds* - E. R. Blake

## Rufous-breasted Wood Quail     *Odontophorus speciasus*
                                    (Tshudi 1843)

Subspecies:

| | |
|---|---|
| *O.s.soederstroemis* (Lonnberg & Radahl 1922) | E. Ecuador |
| *O.s.speciosus* (Tschudi 1843) | Eastern & Central Peru |
| *O.s.loricatus* (Todd 1932) | S.E. Peru, Eastern Bolivia |

### Habitat
Lowland forest

### Description
Adult 9¾"-10½" (250-265mm) in length. Sexes different. Male - top of head deep brown or dusky chestnut, forehead and lateral border of the crown black, more or less speckled white; ear coverts dull chestnut or dusky; throat, sides of head and sides of neck black, upper parts mainly brown, finely vermiculated black, the mantle and back often streaked with white, scapulars and back spotted with black and buff; wing coverts often spotted with white or buff; flight feathers fuscous, the secondaries vermiculated with rufous, breast, abdomen and sides rufous chestnut; lower flanks and belly brown, often barred with buff and black, eyes brown, bill black, feet and bare skin around eyes blue black. Female - similar to male, excepting foreneck and upper breast alone rufous, the rear underparts dark grey.

### Distribution
Eastern Eucador, South in Eastern and Central Peru to Northern and Eastern Bolivia

**Reference:** *Manual of Neotropical Birds* - E.R. Blake

## Gorgeted Wood Quail

*Odontophorus strophium*
(Gould 1844)

Subspecies:
None known

### Habitat
Temperate zone of the Eastern Andes

### Description
Adults 10" (255mm) in length. Sexes different. Male - crown and ear coverts brown, superciliary stripe, molar area and the chin white, more or less speckled black, throat and bar across upper chest black, interrupted by a white band across forehead; uppersurface mainly brown, mottled and spotted scapulars black, the mantle finely streaked white; undersurface of body rufous chestnut, streaked and spotted white. Bill black, feet pale olive. Female - similar excepting dark grey below.

### Distribution
Eastern Andes of Colombia

**Reference:** *Manual of Neotropical Birds* - E. R. Blake

## Tacaruna Wood Quail — *Odontophorus dialeucos*
(Wetmore 1963)

Subspecies:
None known

### Habitat
Humid forest in sub-tropical zone

### Description
Adults 8½"-10" (220-250mm) in length. Sexes essentially alike. Male - pileum black, minutely seckled with white, lores and superciliaries white, rear extension and behind neck cinnamon buff, white of chin and foreneck separated by the expansive black of the throat, upperparts dark brownish olive, mottled and vermiculated with black and cinnamon; tertials boldly spotted with black, undersurface of body tawny brown to dusky olive, finely vermiculated with black and cinnamon, bill and feet black.

### Distribution
Southern end of the Serrania del Darien, extreme Eastern Panama

**Reference:** *Manual of Neotropical Birds* - E.R. Blake

## Venezuelan Wood Quail   *Odontophorus columbianus*
(Gould 1850)

Subspecies:
None known

**Habitat**
Subtropical zone

**Description**
Adults 11"-12" (280-300mm) in length. Sexes different. Male - uppersurface similar to *O.atrifrous* and *O.strophium*, but hindneck rufous, mixed with black, upper tail coverts more reddish, and primaries uniform fuscous. Chin and throat white streaked with black, especially laterally; ear coverts, sides of neck, and barred across foreneck, black mixed with chestnut; underparts brown, dullest rear, the breast and sides with prominent diamond-shaped white spots, edged with black. Bill black, feet grey. Female - similar to male, but pale shaft streaks of mantle and back less developed or lacking; breast and sides uniform grey brown, without white spots or black markings.

**Distribution**
Venezuela in South-Western Tachina and the Coast range from Carabobo to Miranda.

**Reference:** *Manual of Neotropical Birds* - E.R.Blake

# Black-breasted or White-throated Wood Quail

*Odontophorus leucolaemus*
(Salvin 1867)

### Habitat
Humid forest, upper tropical and sub-tropical zone

### Description
Adults 9"-10" (230-250mm) in length. Sexes similar. Above dark cinnamon brown, finely vermiculated with black, scapulars and tertials boldly spotted with black, remiges fuscous brown, the outer webs of the secondaries vermiculated with cinnamon and black, forehead and sides of head mainly black, the former speckled with white; throat more or less extensively white, sometimes much restricted by black and white spotting below eyes and auriculars; foreneck and breast black, the latter barred white or with scattered white-tipped feathers; rear underparts deep cinnamon brown, minutely vermiculated with black, eyes brown, bill black, feet plumbeous.

### Distribution
Northern and Eastern Costa Rica, South to Western Panama in Bocas del Toro, Chiniqui and Veraguas

**Reference:** *Manual of Neotropical Birds* - E.R. Blake

5:23

## Stripe-faced Wood Quail
*Odontophorus balliviani*
(Gould 1846)

**Habitat**
Heavy forest, sub-tropical zone

**Description**
Adults 10.4"-11" (260-280mm) in length. Sexes similar. Brown and nape chestnut, a black portocular stripe, bordered above and below by a tawny buff or cinnamon stripe extending forward above eye and chin; uppersurface mainly olive brown or reddish brown, minutely vermiculated with black, scapular and inner secondaries with large black spots on inner webs; flight feathers mottled fuscous and cinnamon, underparts deep chestnut brown, darkest on the throat, the breast, abdomen, sides and flanks with conspicuous white diamond-shaped spots, with black borders. Eyes hazel, bill black, feet dark grey.

**Distribution**
Andes in South Eastern Peru and Northern Bolivia

**Reference:** *Manual of Neotropical Birds* - E. R. Blake

# Starred Wood Quail

*Odontophorus stellatus*
(Gould 1843)

**Habitat**
Tropical zone

**Description**
Adults 9½"-10¼" (240-260mm) in length. Sexes similar. Upper surfaces essentially like *O.gujanensis*, but feathers of occipital crest longer and mainly chestnut rufous, hindhead, sides of head and throat dark ash grey, and superciliary region sometimes finely speckled white; chest and undersurface of body chestnut rufous, more ochraceous medially, the breast and sides of chest sparsely speckled with white, diamond shaped spots; flanks, lower abdomen and under-tail coverts dull reddish brown, sometimes barred with black, bill black (immature reddish orange above, yellowish below), feet brown black.

**Distribution**
Upper Amazonia in Eastern Ecuador and Eastern Peru, Western Brazil South of the Amazon East to the Rio Madeira and Southward to Beni, Northern Bolivia.

**Reference:** *Manual of Neotropical Birds* - E.R.Blake

## Spotted Wood Quail
*Odontophorus guttatus*
(Gould 1838)

**Habitat**
Humid forest, tropical and sub-tropical zones

**Description**
Adults 9"-10½" (230-265mm) in length. Sexes different. Male - brown, deep brown to blackish, the long feathers of the occipital crest bright cinnamon, tipped darker; ear coverts and sides of neck chestnut; hindneck and mantle olive brown or greyish, the shaft streaks white, wings, tail and uppersurfaces of body similar to *O.gujanensis*, throat and foreneck black, finely streaked with white; undersurface olive brown or reddish brown (brightest on breast) with numerous round and elongated white spots - these often with narrow black borders; lower flanks and tail coverts dull cinnamon brown, often barred with black, eye pale brown, bare lores grey, bill dark grey to black, feet dull green Female - similar to male, but crown duller, darker and occipital crest without cinnamon feathers.

**Distribution**
Central America (except El Salvador) from Guatemala, South to the Pacific slope of the extreme Western Panama in Chinqui.

**Reference:** *Manual of Neotropical Birds* - E.R.Blake

Black-throated Bobwhite, ♂
(*Colinus nigrogularis*),

Ocellated Quail, ♂
(*Crytonyx ocellatus*),

Crested Bobwhite, ♂
(*Colinus cristatus*),

Starred Wood-Quail
(*Odontophorus stellatus*),

Buffy-fronted Wood-Partridge
(*Dendrortyx leucophrys*),

Spotted Wood-Quail
(*Odontophorus guttatus*)

Marbled Wood-Quail
(*Odontophorus gujanensis*)

Singing Quail, ♂
(*Dactylortyx thoracicus*)

Tawny-faced Quail, ♂
(*Rhynchortyx cinctus*)

Rufous-fronted Wood-Quail
(*Odontophorus erythrops*)

Plate from the Manual of Neotropical Birds by Emmet R. Blake. University of Chicago Press.

**Californian Quail** ♀
*Callipepla californica*

**Californian Quail** ♂
*Callipepla californica*

**Japanese Quail** ♂
*Coturnix japonica*

**Elegant Quail** ♂
*Callipepla douglasii*

# Singing (or long-toed) Quail     *Dactylortyx thoracicus*
(Gambel 1848)

Subspecies: Approximately seventeen recorded

| | |
|---|---|
| *D.t.sharpei* (Nelson 1903) | - N. Guatemala |
| *D.t.colophorus* (Warner & Hassell) | - Guatemala |
| *D.t.salvadoranus* (Dicky & Van Rossen 1928) | - El Salvador |
| *D.t.taylori* (Van Rossen 1932) | - El Salvador |
| *D.t.fuscus* (Conova 1937) | - Honduras |
| *D.t.rufescens* (Warner & Hassell 1957) | - Honduras |
| *D.t.conoveri* (Warner & Hassell 1957) | - Honduras |

## Habitat

| | |
|---|---|
| *D.t.thoracicus* | Forest, mainly sub-tropical |
| *D.t.sharpei* | Semi-deciduous lowland forest |
| *D.t.colophorus* | Humid forest above 5,000 |
| *D.t.salvadoranus* | Oak association (2,500-4,000ft) of arid upper tropical zone |
| *D.t.taylori* | Oak - coffee association of arid tropical zone |
| *D.t.fuscus* | Cloud forest |
| *D.t.rufescens* | Hardwood cloud forest (4,000-7,000ft) |

## Description

Adults 8¾"-9" (220-230mm) in length. Sexes different. Male - brown, deep brown, usually darker on back; an obscure nuchal collar of buff and black spots; mantle, back and wings mottled brown and grey and with pale shaft streaks; scapulars and inner flight feathers with prominent black spots; primaries fuscous, usually barred with buff on outer webs, lower back and rump greyish or olive brown, sides of head extensively cinnamon rufous, the ear coverts brown or dusky; throat cinnamon rufous or white; foreneck, breast sides, and flanks greyish brown, finely streaked with white; abdomen white; under tail coverts buff, broadly barred with black, eye brown, bill blackish brown, feet plumbeous. Female - similar, but sides of head grey and throat white; breast and sides cinnamon brown, shading to buff on abdomen and flanks.

**Distribution**

Southern Mexico (North to Jalisco and Southern Tamanlipas) Guatemala, El Salvador and Honduras

**Reference:** *Manual of Neotropical Birds* - E.R.Blake

## Mearns Quail

*Cyntonyx Montezumae*
(Vigors 1830)

Harlequin Quail
Montezuma Quail
Painted Quail
Fools Quail
Squat Quail

Subspecies:
*C.m.mearnsi* - Mearns Harlequin Quail
*C.m.merriami* - Merriam Harlequin Quail
*C.m.salli* - Salle Harlequin Quail
*C.m.rowley* - not verified

### Natural Habitat

Drier parts of central highlands, grassy slopes, fields and open pine woodlands between 5,000 - 10,000 feet.

### Description

Adults 8" 9½" (204 242mm) in length. Males have a beautiful facial pattern of black and blue-black and white and a soft tan crest that projects backward and down over the nape, underparts grey to olive brown, extensively spotted and marked with black, white and buff markings, sides and flanks are dark grey with rounded spots of white cinnamon, or rufous brown. Females generally cinnamon-coloured with black markings on back, small buff crest mottled brown and buffy face with whitish chin and throat, back and wings are extensively mottled, underparts mostly buff with black flecks in the abdominal region.

### Distribution

South-Western United States, South to Oaxaco, Mexico (*C.ocellatus* extends from southern Oaxaca to Nicaragua).

### Avicutural notes

Recommended aviary size   48"(1.25m) x 48"(1.25m)

| | |
|---|---|
| Number in captivity | 79 (WPA Census 1978) |
| Egg clutch size | 6-16 eggs |
| Egg colour | white |
| Incubation period | 24-25 days |
| Noise level | limited |
| Habits | prone to fly up vertically and cause injury |
| Food | small crumbs, mixed millet, insectile food, live food |
| Novice selection | difficult, not recommended |
| Special note | rare |

# Ocellated Quail

*Cyntonyx ocellatus*
(Gould 1837)

### Natural habitat
Open pine forest and brushy fields, arid highland up to 7,000 ft.

### Description
Adults 7½"-8" (190-200mm) in length. Sexes different. Male - Forehead and sides of head extensively black and slate blue. The orbital and post-orbital areas white; chin and median throat black, margined laterally and posteriorly with a broad white band, followed by a black band; above mainly grey-olive, the mantle, back and scapulars irregularly blotched, the wings spotted and barred with black, and the whole broadly streaked with buff and chestnut; undersurface mainly ochraceous (breast) and chestnut; sides of breast and mantle - grey, spotted with buff; tibiae and undertail coverts black. Eyes dark brown, bill black and pale blue; feet light blue. Female - uppersurface vinaceous brown, vermiculated and barred black, mantle, back and wing coverts conspicuously striped with buff, throat and superciliary stripe white, more or less speckled and barred with black; an indistinct black collar; below vinaceous, sparsely spotted and barred with black.

**Reference:** *Manual of Neotropical Birds* - E. R. Blake

### Distribution
Guatemala, East of the Pacific Divide, Southward in the Cordillera of El Salvador and Honduras to Northern Nicaragua.

**Reference:** Dicky and Van Rossen 1938. *Bds. El Salvador* pp 155.56

## Tawny-faced Quail

*Rhynchortyx cinctus*
(Ogilvie-Grant 1893)

Subspecies:
*R.c.pudibundus* - Peters 1929. Honduras, NE Nicaragua
*R.c.circtus* - Salvin 1876. Costa Rica, Panama
*R.c.australis* - Chapman 1915. Colombia, NW Ecuador

### Habitat
Deep forest of the tropical zone

### Description
Adults 7½"-8" (190-200mm) in length. Sexes different. Male - brown and hind neck deep brown, forehead and sides of head cinnamon rufous; a dark eyestripe; mantle and upper back dark grey; the feathers edged or tipped brown, lower back, rump and upper tail coverts grey, tinged buff, finely streaked and speckled with black; scapulars black, mottled with cinnamon, wing coverts grey, tipped black on inner webs; remiges fuscous, the outer secondaries mottled cinnamon on outer webs; throat white or whitish, shading to bluish grey on breast, lower breast and sides tawny buff, abdomen white, eyes brown, bill and feet bluish grey. Female - uppersurface similar to male, but mantle, rump and upper tail coverts much browner; a fine white stripe above ear coverts; sides of head, foreneck and breast dull reddish brown; upper throat and rear underparts white, the latter barred black.

### Distribution
Caribbean slope of Honduras, Nicaragua, Costa Rica, and Panama to extreme North-Western Colombia and North-Western Ecuador.

**Reference:** *Manual of Neotropical Birds* - E.R.Blake

5:30

## Eurasian Quail

*Coturnix coturnix*
(Linnaeus 1766)

Common Quail
European Quail
Migratory Quail

Subspecies
*C.c.africana* - African Quail
*C.c.confisa* - Madeira Quail
*C.c.capensis* - Cape Quail

**Natural habitat**

A migratory bird, moving south in September and October to warmer climates, returning in March and April. Found in grassland and cornfields.

**Description**

Adults 6½"-7½" (165-192mm) in length. Head warm buff with two dark lines from beak to nape and with a prominent white eyebrow stripe and short, dark moustache marks; cheeks warm brown, throat pale buff, both outlined with a dark brown stripe from ear coverts, meeting under chin where it forms a black patch, upper parts dark brown striated with buff and faintly mottled with black, breast and flanks reddish-brown flecked with black or dark brown and striated on the flanks with white marks; belly white or pale buff, tail brown, but very short, concealed by rain-like feathers of the rump; bill and legs pale yellow, eye dark brown. Female - slightly larger than the male, less distinctly marked, lacking in the dark band and patch on throat.

**Distribution**

Europe, Asia, Africa.

**Avicultural notes**

| | |
|---|---|
| Recommended aviary size | 48"(1.25m) x 48"(1.25m) |
| Number in captivity | 602 (WPA Census 1978) |
| Egg clutch size | 10-12 eggs |
| Egg colour | creamy-white or buff, blotched and spotted with rich brown |
| Incubation period | 18 days |
| Noise level | reasonable call |
| Habits | ground dwelling, excessively wild, apt to fly up at night |
| Food | mixed millet, chick crumbs, greenfood, little live food |
| Novice selection | not suitable, too restless |
| Special note | Male must be removed as soon as eggs are laid to allow hen to brood, hen will not sit if in calling distance of male |

## Japanese Quail

*Coturnix japonica*
(Perry 1856)

### Natural habitat
Grassland, cornfield, cultivation

### Description
Adults 5½"-6" (140-153mm) in length. As common Quail, *coturnix coturnix* except males have the chin and throat dull brick red, devoid of any black markings, others have only the upper two thirds of the throat dull red and the lower white; while a third type have in addition a black band down the middle of the red part. Margins of the flank-feathers mostly rufous and much less spotted with black. Female - differs, having the chin and throat feathers elongated and pointed especially on the sides and generally margined with rufous, the chest and sides less spotted with black.

### Distribution
South-East Asia. Migrant up to 4,000 feet in Burma, NW Thailand, N. and Central Ammam; Tonkin, N. Laos, Hong Kong.

### Avicultural notes

| | |
|---|---|
| Recommended aviary size | 48"(1.25m) x 48"(1.25m) |
| Number in captivity | 978 (WPA Census) |
| Egg clutch size | 10-12 eggs |
| Egg colour | Cream-white or buff, boldly blotched and spotted rich brown |
| Incubation period | 18 days |
| Noise level | reasonable |
| Habits | ground dwelling |
| Food | mixed millets, chick crumbs, greenfood |
| Novice selection | ideal |
| Special note | Now hybrids in many forms therefore true form difficult to establish. Produced in large numbers for the table. See - The Coturnix Laying Quails for identification. |

## Rain Quail

*Coturnix coromandelica*
(Bonn 1791)

Black-breasted Quail

**Natural habitat**
Open grassland and cultivated areas

**Description**
Adults 6"(153mm) in length. Male - centre of head chestnut with two black lines from base of beak to nape, white eyebrow marks and a dark line through the eye; cheeks and throat white, margined with black, upper parts russet, heavily streaked with buff and dark brown; upper parts pale chestnut striated with black and a large black mark in the centre of the breast. Female - lacks the black marks on head, chin and breast and the buff striations on the upper parts are much less conspicuous.

**Distribution**
India, Ceylon, Burma to the Shan States

**Avicultural notes**

| | |
|---|---|
| Recommended aviary size | 39"(1m) x 39"(1m) |
| Number in captivity | 53 (WPA Census 1978) |
| Egg clutch size | 10-12 eggs |
| Egg colour | yellowish-white to brown buff with blackish or brown spotting |
| Incubation period | 17 days |
| Noise level | reasonable |
| Habits | prone to fly upwards |
| Food | 20% chick crumbs, plus small millet and maw seed |
| Novice selection | suitable |
| Special note | protect from frost in winter |

5:33

## Harlequin Quail
*Coturnix delegorguei*
(Ogilvie-Grant 1893)

### Natural habitat
Open grasslands and cultivated areas

### Description
Adults 6½"(165mm) in length. Male - black-brown with a lighter centre stripe, a black stripe runs through the eye extending behind the ear coverts; a white stripe runs above the eye to nape; cheeks and throat white with a black band across the cheeks, which continues down the front and encircles the throat. The breast is black in the centre with red-brown stripes running lengthwise to the sides; belly and under-tail coverts brown-red, upper parts black-brown with small lighter cross stripes with long yellow stripes over the scapulars and back. Female - black as well as white markings on head and throat are non-existent; throat whitish, the remainder of the underparts brown with light margins and paler black markings.

### Distribution
Africa, South of about 15 degrees North latitude

### Avicultural notes

| | |
|---|---|
| Recommended aviary size | 39"(1m) x 39"(1m) |
| Number in captivity | 119 (WPA Census 1978) |
| Egg clutch size | 6-8 eggs |
| Egg colour | olive white or cream buff, blotches of chestnut, sepia, black |
| Incubation period | 17 days |
| Noise level | reasonable |
| Habits | ground-dwelling, can be kept with other birds |
| Food | 20% protein chick crumbs, mixed millet little live food |
| Novice selection | suitable |
| Special note | males prone to fight own sex if housed together |

## Chinese Painted Quail       *Excalfactoria chinensis*
(Linnaeus 1766)

King Quail (1)
Blue breasted Quail (2)

Subspecies:

(1) *E.chinensis lineata* Ogilvie-Grant 1893 Australia
    *E.lepida* Hartlarb 1879.             New Guinea
(2) *E.adansonii* Ogilvie-Grant 1893     Africa

**Natural habitat**
Open swampy grasslands or meadows, low bush jungle, edges of low-standing crops

**Description**
Adults 4½"-5" (114-127 mm) in length. Male - upper parts brown mottled with black and a blackish forehead, cheeks white outlined by a black line extending from the back, below the eyes and joining the black throat, broad white band across upper breast, extending backwards to the sides of neck and also outlined in black, chest and flanks blue-grey, breast and belly deep chestnut, eyes hazel, beak black, legs yellow. Female - lacks the black and white on head and upper breast also blue-grey on chest and flanks, her colour is generally dull brown, mottled on upper parts, paler on the breast.
*E.c.lineata:* somewhat darker and more strongly marked subspecies, southern representative found in Australia.
*E.adamsonii:* males differ from *E.chinensis* in having the upper parts blackish brown worked with slate; the upper tail coverts and wing coverts chestnut, the latter with slate-grey stripes, underparts dark slate-grey, except sides and flanks, which are bright chestnut.
Domestic mutations - fawn, silver, white.

Distribution
India, South-East China, Thailand, Indo-China, Ceylon, Haiman Formosa, New Guinea, South Africa, Australia.

Avicutural notes

| | |
|---|---|
| Recommended aviary size | 39"(1m) x 39"(1m) |
| Number in captivity | Many bred in each year |
| Egg clutch size | 6-12 eggs |
| Egg colour | olive-brown |
| Incubation period | 16 days |
| Noise level | low, soft double whistle note |
| Habits | ground-dwelling species |
| Food | fine seed, millets, chick crumbs, maw seed, little live food |
| Novice selection | ideal for the beginner |
| Special note | chicks capable of creeping through ½" mesh wire, small water troughs required to prevent drowning of chicks. |

## Pectoral Quail

*Coturnix pectoralis*
(Gould 1837)

Stubble Quail
Australian Quail

**Natural habitat**
   Pastures, grassland, stubble fields

**Description**
   Adults 7" (178mm) in length. Male - differs from male *C.coturnix* chiefly in having the sides of the head, chin and throat dull brick red (as in *C.japonica*), but feathers of the underparts are white with black shaft stripes and there is a black patch in the middle of chest. Female - as *C.coturnix*, except feathers of chest and breast longitudinally barred with black near extremes, the bars being interrupted in the middle by a wide buff interface.

**Distribution**
   Australia, Eastern and South-Eastern Australia, Tasmania.

**Avicultural notes**

| | |
|---|---|
| Recommended aviary size | 48"(1.25m) x 48"(1.25m) |
| Number in captivity | 41 (WPA Census 1978) |
| Egg clutch size | 7-14 eggs |
| Egg colour | ground colour yellowish-white, flecked with umber-brown to large blotches of a darker tint |
| Incubation period | 18 days |
| Noise level | reasonable |
| Habits | ground dwelling |
| Food | mixed millets, small grain, crumbs, greenstuff, a little live food |
| Novice selection | possible |
| Special note | during winter best kept under cover |

5:36

## New Zealand Quail *Coturnix novae-zealandise* (Buller 1888)

(considered possibly extinct now)

**Natural habitat**
Open country and grass covered downs

**Description**
Adults 6"-7" (152-178mm) in length. Male - as *C.pectoralis*, the general colour of the upper parts warmer in tone; the forepart of the neck is mostly black like the middle of the breast. Female - as *C.pectoralis*, except for the black bars on the chest and breast feathers are confluent and the markings on rest of underparts are more numerous.

**Distribution**
New Zealand

## Brown Quail

*Synoicus ypsilophous*
(Temminck 1815)

Australian Swamp Quail
Tasmanian Brown Quail
Tasmanian Silou Quail

Subspecies:
*S.y.australis* Gould 1843. -Australia, Tasmania
*S.y.raaltenic* Ogilvie-Grant 1893 -Is. of Timor
*S.y.plumbeous* Salvadori 1894. -SE New Guinea

**Natural habitat**
Grassy flats and damp spots overgrown with undergrowth in the vicinity of rivers and waterholes

**Description**
Adults 7"-8½" (178-213mm) in length. Male - upperparts are reddish-brown with dull grey centres, the black mottlings are few and fine, and the white shafts so conspicuous in younger birds are scarcely visible. Sides of head and throat dull grey, underparts buff with grey centres and almost devoid of black cross-bars. Upperparts are mottled with black, barred with rufous, narrow white shafts of the feathers being well defined; sides of the head and throat pale vinaceous white, remaining underparts buff, with V shaped black cross bars. Female - chiefly brown, spotted and streaked with black and the feathers of the back having white stripes. Bill horn-coloured, black towards tip, legs are pale yellow.

**Distribution**
Australia, Southern Queensland, New South Wales, Victoria, introduced to New Zealand, Tasmania, SE New Guinea, Is. of Timor and Flores.

**Avicultural notes**
Recommended aviary size  48"(1.25m) x 48"(1.25m)
Number in captivity  31 (WPA Census 1978)

5:38

**Chinese Painted Quail** ♀ ♂
*Excalfactoria chinensis*

**Gambel's Quail** ♂
*Callipepla gambelii*

**Gambel's Quail** ♀
*Callipepla gambelii*

# The Coturnix Laying Quails Identification Chart

**MALE PHARAOH D1**
MPD1

**FEMALE PHARAOH D1**
FDP1

**MALE MANCHURIAN GOLDEN**
MMCH

**FEMALE MANCHURIAN GOLDEN**
FMCH

**FEMALE BRITISH RANGE**
FBRG

**FEMALE ENGLISH WHITE**
FEWT

**FEMALE TUXEDO**
FTUX

This chart pair at Marsh Farm Robert Richer

Sex can be determined in the Pharaoh and Manchurian bre by subtle differences in breast colour. The colour distinct becomes apparent by the time the birds are two weeks old. these two breeds, males have unbroken brown coloured brea that are darker at the top, under the white neck band, and f lighter downward. Pharaoh and Manchurian hens have gre breasts interspersed with dark specking. The British Ran English White and Tuxedo breeds have no sex colour dif ences. After breeding and laying starts in all breeds, the ma tend to lose weight but hens maintain their size or gain un their weight is approximately 20% greater than that of males. Laying hens are generally plumper in appearance th breeding males. Both sexes are substantially the same size fore they begin breeding.

Reproduced by kind permission of Marsh Farms.

| | |
|---|---|
| Egg clutch size | 10-18 eggs |
| Egg colour | Green or bluish-white, finely dotted all over with light brown |
| Incubation period | 18 days |
| Noise level | loud whistle-like note, heard at daybreak and dusk |
| Habits | timid, but will tame down |
| Food | mixed millet, chick crumbs, insectile food, greenstuff |
| Novice selection | not recommended |
| Special note | should be kept inside during winter |

## Snow Mountain Quail     *Anmophosis monorthonyx*
(Van Oort 1910)

**Natural habitat**
Edge of the tree line, areas of tall grass and bushes, to the limits of shorter grass on more barren ridges.

**Description**
Adults 10"-11"(255-280mm) in length. Male - blackish-brown upper-parts, with buffish to rufous bars and narrow shaft streaks; the throat and lateral aspects of the neck are light chestnut, with forehead and face buff, the underparts are rich brown with conspicuous irregular black bars on the upper breast, flanks and undertail coverts. Female - similar, but with heavier black barring on paler buff underparts, with darker brown and less conspicuous bars and paler shaft stripes on upper-parts, eyes dark brown, bill horn-colour with yellow base, feet pale yellow.

**Distribution**
Oranje Mountain slopes at 10,000-13,000 feet in New Guinea.

# Indian Mountain Quail

*Ophrysia superciliosa*
(Bonep 1856)

**Natural habitat**
Thick grass - jungle and brushwood

**Description**
Adults 8.8"-9" (215-230mm) in length. Male - middle of crown and nape brownish-grey, with black shaft-stripes; sides of crown black; forehead and a wide band down each side of the crown white; sides of the head, chin and throat black, with a white band on each side of the latter, upper and under parts grey, the former washed with olive-brown and all the feathers edged with black, under tail coverts black, tipped and spotted with white. Eyes - red, legs - red-orange, bill - yellow. Female - upper parts, brown most of the feathers with black shaft stripes or blotches; a black band on each side of the crown, eyebrow-stripes and sides of the head vinous-grey, throat white, under-parts similar to the back, but paler and more tawny.

**Distribution**
North-Western India in the neighborhood of Masuni and Naimi Tel.

## Jungle Bush Quail

*Perdicula asiatica*
(Latham 1790)

### Natural habitat
Moderately thick forests and jungle, hills and ravines.

### Description
Adults 6¼" (159mm) in length. Male - upperparts brown, with pale buff shaft stripes on the backs, and black bars and blotches on the scapulars and wing coverts; forehead, eyebrow stripes and throat rufous-chestnut with whitish edges; underparts white, with regular black cross-bars; inner webs of primary flight feathers not barred with rufous-buff. Female - throat rufous-chestnut like the male, but no buff shaft-streaks on the upper parts and the underparts uniform vinaceous-buff.

### Distribution
India and Ceylon

### Avicultural notes

| | |
|---|---|
| Recommended aviary size | 48"(1.25m) x 48"(1.25m) |
| Number in captivity | 21 (WPA Census 1978) |
| Egg clutch size | 5-7 eggs |
| Egg colour | creamy to brown white |
| Incubation period | 21 days |
| Noise level | reasonable |
| Habits | ground dwelling |
| Food | small millet, maw seed, hard boiled egg, chick crumbs |
| Novice selection | possible if available |
| Special note | good breeder in captivity |

## Rock Bush Quail  *Perdicula argoondah*
(Hume & Marshall 1879)

Red Bush Quail

### Natural habitat
Dry, rocky plains, low hillocks, scattered thornbushes and barren sparsely-cultivated land.

### Description
Adults 6½" (165mm) in length. Male - similar to male *P.asiatica*, but upper-parts barred with buff and black or grey; the rufous on the throat is dull brick colour, not bordered white; and the quills are barred on the inner as well as the outer webs with rufous buff. Female - has the throat white, tinged with vinaceous; the upper-parts vinaceous-brown and underparts dull vinaceous, a few faint buff and dusky markings on the middle of the belly of whitish buff.

### Distribution
India, Ceylon, introduced Mauritius

### Avicultural notes
| | |
|---|---|
| Recommended aviary size | 48"(1.25m) x 48"(1.25m) |
| Number in captivity | 6 (WPA Census 1978) |
| Egg clutch size | 5-7 eggs |
| Egg colour | glossy white, slightly tinged with brownish-buff |
| Incubation period | 21 days |
| Noise level | reasonable |
| Habits | ground dwelling |
| Food | small millet, maw seed, chick crumbs, green food |
| Novice selection | possible if available |

## Painted Bush Quail

*Perdicula erythrorhyncha*
(Sykes 1834)

Subspecies
*P.c.blewitti* (Hume 1874) Central India

**Natural habitat**
Found on outskirts of dense cover, high grass, dense clumps of fern or rocky ground, also near cultivated areas

**Description**
Adults 7" (178mm) in length. Male - colour earthy-brown, with rounded black spots, blotched, especially on the wings with black together with whitish shaft-streaks and buff cross bars; top of head, except the middle of crown, black with a narrow well-defined white band between the eyes, continuing backwards on each side of the head, forming a U shaped white mark; throat white, chest grey brown with light rufous, shading to rufous-chestnut on the rest of the underparts, sides and flanks with rather large black white edged spots. Female - like male, but the black on head and white throat replaced by dull rufous-chestnut.

**Distribution**
South-Western hills of the Peninsula of India, extending from Bombay to the Cardamum Hills in Travancore.

**Avicultural notes**

| | |
|---|---|
| Recommended aviary size | 48"(1.25m) x 48"(1.25m) |
| Number in captivity | 9 (WPA Census 1978) |
| Egg clutch size | 10-12 eggs |
| Egg colour | glossy pale brownish buff |
| Incubation period | 21 days |
| Noise level | reasonable |
| Habits | ground dwelling |
| Food | small millets, chick crumbs, green food |
| Novice selection | possible, if available |

## Manipur Bush Quail

*Perdicula Monipurensis*
(Hume 1880)

Natural habitat
    Lives in almost inpenetrable patches of elephant grass, only venturing into the open to feed.

Description
    Adults 6½" (165mm) in length. Male - upper-parts dark grey, barred and blotched on the wings with black, forehead eyebrow-stripes and throat dark chestnut, neck and chest grey, shading into tawny on the rest of the underparts, which have a black shaft-stripe and wide black cross bar on each feather. Female - differs from the male in having no chestnut on the head or throat, the latter being whitish, and the breast and belly are buff.

Distribution
    Sikhim and South-Eastern Manipur Hills

**Reference:** *Hand-book of the Game Birds* - W.R. Ogilvie-Grant

# CHAPTER 6

## BREEDING REQUIREMENTS

### Health

Internal parasites and worms, such as gapes or gizzard worm are a common cause of infertility and birds may appear to be in good condition, but could well have some underlying disease which makes them infertile. Worms will reduce a bird's food uptake, therefore all your birds should be wormed regularly. Avian tuberculosis, aspergillosis, coccidiosis are common infections where birds are kept on the same ground for years, and birds with deformed legs or feet can prevent successful mating.

A watch must be kept for signs of external parasites, fleas, lice, mites, etc., as they can become a constant irritation and affect the health of your birds. There are many brands of insecticide available on the market today which are completely harmless; one's birds should be treated before each breeding season.

### Nutrition

Inadequate and poor quality food can affect fertility and in extreme cases the hen birds just do not lay eggs. and those which do could well be infertile. The same applies to the cock birds which are unable to fertilise them. Therefore, a balanced diet is most important if success is to be achieved.

### Fertility

As a general rule, Quail are good for four to seven years, but the age of the male has a major influence on fertility and the resultant young stock, and although your birds may show that they are sexually mature, it does not mean you will automatically obtain the results you expect; good husbandry is all important. Quail can be classed as an exotic species, and therefore most breeders continue to set eggs even when their birds are old whereas domestic species are usually disposed of when fertility falls.

### Environment

The housing should be adequate for the species of Quail to be kept and a guide to their respective requirements is mentioned in Chapter 5. Protection from extremes of temperature and rainfall are all important, as is access to clean water at all times. Should the pens become very muddy, this can in turn cause a build-up of disease. Light and temperature stimulates breeding conditions, but it is not synchronised in the male and the female at the same time. Over the years I have considered the possibility of force breeding rare birds to obtain the maximum number in a season, but conclude that it is far better to obtain a few good and healthy youngsters, rather than a lot of weaklings which will become degenerate stock in the future.

### In-Breeding

Birds tend to be weaker, lack vigour, and hence poor display. The cocks produce only small quantities of inferior sperm; also it can be the fault of the hen or the cock when the germ dies before development, giving every appearance of an infertile egg. New blood or breeding to another strain has the opposite effect, it gives vigour, for as each bird has its own recessive traits, so the dominant aspects of both parents appear in their young.

### Stress

Pen management and bad environment is one of the main causes of stress. Pens which are too small or having poor light can again give poor results. Quail which spend their time running up and down the wire of their pens cannot be expected to give fertile eggs. The presence of potential predators, such as cats, dogs and children will not allow your birds to settle to produce good results. Another aspect is the bullying by fellow birds. It is always preferable to house only one pair of each species and to have suitable solid partitions between pairs, as the male birds will constantly run up and down the wire trying to fight with his next door counterpart, then mating with his hen bird to show dominance.

In general Quail are monogamous and will only mate with one hen, leaving the remaining hens infertile. Therefore, caution should be taken when running trios together; perhaps the Japanese *(Coturnix japonica)* and the Chinese Painted Quail *( E. chinensis )* could be the exception (although have recently seen groups of six pairs or more successfully breeding in the U.S.A. and Canada).

### Stock
The age of the parents has a marked influence on the hatchability; eggs from very young birds give a poor hatch rate from either weak germs or immaturity. Most Quail are sexually mature in their first year, but one does not normally obtain really good results until the second year.

### Housing
The birds must be housed in an area suitable for each species, taking into account such features as its natural habitat, time of year, weather conditions, temperature, and the amount of light available. Birds must be clean and, above all, contented.

### Conditions
As already stressed, one cannot expect to obtain good breeding results if your stock is housed in cold, draughty pens, with no shelter from the elements. Even in the wild you will see game birds sheltering against high winds and heavy rain, therefore, your captive stock will expect to do the same.

### Laying season
If your birds are housed outside throughout the year, most species will start to lay in late April or early May, being stimulated by the warmer weather and longer days. They then may well continue until late July or mid August, again dependent on the weather. However, if your birds are housed inside, it is most likely they will show signs of breeding and start laying much earlier in the year. As previously mentioned this is not advisable, due to the possibility of obtaining poor stock.

## Egg eating

Should you find egg eating becoming a problem, use an old country method of overcoming this. Take an egg similar to the bird's own, blow out its contents and fill with ordinary household mustard, and place where the birds would normally lay. The bird concerned will soon find it, and quickly go off the idea. Alternatively, obtain a china or wooden egg of the same size and shape, and your bird will soon become disinterested.

## Temperature

Variations in temperature will also affect your egg production. As with inadequate light, the effect may not be enough to reduce the number of eggs laid, but could well affect the hatchability.

## Light

Most birds are stimulated into breeding by change in the duration of light; the metabolism of both sexes changes, as well as the reproductive organs. Therefore, the lack of light can reduce the stimulation, resultant detriment to the egg, or indeed no eggs at all !!

## Natural Food

Food compounders do try extremely hard to produce a diet similar to that in the wild, and include all the elements possible to produce strong and healthy birds. However, it is an undoubted fact that birds housed in an area where there is natural food, such as berries, seeds and insects, increase the hatchability of their eggs. Unfortunately, most breeders cannot afford to have large planted pens for one pair of small Quail; apart from the parasitic infection which Quail are very prone to acquire. Therefore, to keep one's birds on sand or wire floors will eliminate the problems of infection; a good, formulated food, together with a constant supply of clean water, will give extremely good results. They will enjoy clean berries or green food given in season.

## Keeping of Records

It is always very useful to record the number of eggs laid by each pair of birds and the results obtained. This will enable you to see which birds are giving a good hatch rate, and those which are not and require attention. As a routine if you mark each egg laid with the date and a code for each pair of a certain species, it will enable you to keep track of the eggs during incubation. Use one of those markers now available to mark food destined for the freezer, these are non toxic and unaffected by damp, do not press too hard - eggs are fragile. Also record the same information in a book against each breeding pair.

Storage of Eggs

Quail normally lay large clutches of eggs in the wild and have no trouble in storing them. The first eggs laid can often be well over two weeks old before the hen will start to sit, yet hatch just as well as the last egg laid. The same eggs correctly stored and then placed in an incubator should achieve a similar hatch rate. However, if given to a bantam the hatch is normally the same as with the parent bird. There is some evidence that if eggs which are to be stored for some length of time are periodically warmed up to 80°F (26.6°C), for a few minutes each day, combined with turning, the hatch rate will improve. This is what the mother bird does to her own eggs during the time she is waiting to make up a complete clutch, also she rubs natural oils from her feathers on these, which helps to clean the eggs and gives the eggs a covering of lysozyne, which acts as a barrier against infection. This is one point in favour of using a broody bantam over an incubator.

Growth within an egg will recommence if stored at a temperature above 70°F (21.1°C); this growth will be very slow and weak. If prolonged, the embryo will either die or be so weak that it will not survive major growth later in its development. Prolonged periods of cold will also cause death.

The size of the air cell can be used to establish the quality of an egg. Large air cells usually denote eggs which have been badly stored.

All species of eggs are best stored at about 55°F (12.7°C). Fluctuations of temperature can be very damaging, giving poor results.

Egg Storage Humidity

The best temperature and humidity for the storage of eggs is 55°F (12.7°C) at between 75% and 85% humidity. Too low can mean evaporation of the egg contents, and if higher, water will condense within the shell allowing bacteria and moulds to form, thus destroying the embryo.

## Storage Time

Ideally, eggs should not be kept for more than a week, progeny from eggs stored for longer periods tend to produce smaller chicks and will take longer to hatch. This is where an incubator has advantages, as eggs can be set once they are cooled after laying, providing you have adequate rearing facilities when they hatch.

Best results are always achieved by setting fresh eggs.

## Turning of Eggs

Eggs held in storage should be turned twice a day. The reason for this is the yolk tends to float to the highest part of the egg, and if left in contact for any length of time, can stick to the shell, thus preventing development. The eggs are best stored either on their side or large end up.

## Damaged Eggs

Should an egg be cracked and too valuable to discard; the cracks, providing they are not too large, can be painted with nail varnish to prevent excess evaporation and bacteria entering. However, one must be prepared to hatch malformed chicks if care is not taken.

## Candling of Eggs

Infertile eggs can seriously affect the chances of hatching the remaining eggs, therefore, all your eggs should be candled between four and seven days; that is to say, the egg is placed over a bright light, preferably housed in a box with a ½"(125mm) hole in the top, over which the egg is placed, for a very short time. The light will illuminate the contents of the shell showing the embryo as a black dot, surrounded by small blood vessels. Always if in doubt, leave the egg to incubate a little longer. Should the egg be completely clear, remove. You are able to see whether the humidity is too high or low by the air sac in the end of the egg.

### Hatching by Parents

The parent bird is by far the best method of incubating eggs. Her natural ability far outweighs any mechanised devices, being able to turn the eggs when required, having kept them at the correct temperature, to finally hatching them.

However, there are certain pitfalls, such as whether the hen bird will be able to sit undisturbed for the incubation period, the siting of the nest away from direct sunlight, and finally, the pen in which she has nested is secure against the young escaping through the wire, or conversely, vermin entering; both can be a hazard to the chicks.

If at all possible however, this method of breeding Quail must be encouraged, as the progeny will be so much stronger than those bred artificially. Also they retain the instinct to breed naturally, which is so important when holding captive stock, for eventual re-introduction back to the wild.

### Hatching by Bantam

Before the modern electric incubator became popular, the broody bantam was the traditional way of rearing game birds. This method, as with hatching by the parent bird, has its merits, as it is the nearest way of producing chicks naturally. Selection of the bantam is most important; she should be small and compact, to accommodate what are extremely small chicks when first hatched, and should you contemplate placing valuable eggs or chicks under her, you must at least have some knowledge of how she has performed in previous years. It is not unknown for a broody to decide to stand up on her eggs, and allow them to become cold for no real reason. She can become restless due to lice or fleas, and then tread on her eggs, breaking them in the process. Before actually giving her the eggs she is to incubate it is always wise to test whether she is going to sit tight, therefore place some dummy eggs under her for a few days to be quite sure, before committing the more valuable eggs.

### Sitting Box

For a broody to successfully hatch her eggs, she must have peace and quiet. If she is placed in darkness, or limited light to sit, this will improve her steadiness during incubation. A box measuring

12"(305mm) square inside measurement and approximately the same height should be quite adequate for one small broody. If the box is too large, she will probably move around and the eggs will roll away from her, becoming chilled. The reverse if too small - she will be too cramped and uncomfortable, which will make her restless. The front of the box can have a door which closes down, or a piece of sacking which is secured at the top, and held in place at the bottom by two bricks. The box must, of course, have some ventilation, a row of ½"(12.5mm) holes around the top of the box will be quite satisfactory.

Incubators

During the last few years, there have been major advances in the design and understanding of small incubators.

The latest electrically powered models now use a solid state temperature control unit rather than the old capsule which operated the micro-switch to control the temperature and the variations this incurred.

The early incubators are heated by use of paraffin; the machine having a traditional oil heater attached to its side, which has a metal chimney with two outlets, one at the top and the other on the side entering the top of the egg chamber of the incubator. Mounted on the topmost outlet is a damper, which when raised allows the heat generated by the oil heater to escape. When lowered it diverts the hot air into the top of the incubator. A small capsule positioned within the egg chamber expands and contracts as the temperature rises and falls; this in turn regulates the heat. As Quail eggs are small, there is no need to discuss the larger types of incubator on the market. The requirements of the average breeder can be quite adequately catered for by one of the small electrically operated machines currently available, which have a single layer capacity up to 240 eggs at one time.

Should you own one of these older models, it is well worth keeping the operating instructions, as they do need adjustment from time to time.

There are two basic types of electrically operated incubator available: the still air or convection type, and the moving air incubator. The first type has a heater element in the top of the machine, and as the heated air cools, it passes through the eggs and out through the air vents at the sides of the machine just below the heater elements. In the case of the moving air type, it is similar in construction but having a small fan to circulate the air around the eggs. The fan and heater in both types are controlled by a micro switch operated by a capsule, similar to those used in the paraffin incubators. Now with the solid state control, the temperature is no longer controlled by the rise and fall within a capsule and a mass of levers to transmit the result, but an electrical component which senses variations of temperature within itself which in turn operates a switch to the heater, thus a much greater accuracy can be obtained.

My own success over the years has been achieved by using a small still, air machine with the eggs being hand-turned and sprayed with water twice a day. Of course, there are also machines available which will turn your eggs automatically, thus eliminating the time having to be spent on what can be a very boring job. In addition, there is a trend for manufacturers to produce machines with clear tops or covers, so that the eggs can be viewed at all times.

### Humidity Control

There are usually water trays placed in the bottom of most incubators today, which require regular topping up with water to maintain the required humidity. Later models have a drip feed water supply system into the trays.

### Temperatures for Quail

Depending on the type of incubator, one wants to achieve a temperature of around $101°$-$102°F$ ($38.8°C$) on the upper surfaces of the eggs. I suggest you make a note of the maker's instructions to obtain the same result. My own still air incubators run at this temperature.

### Siting of the Incubator

Best results can be obtained when the incubator is positioned out of direct sunlight and in a room where the temperature does not exceed $60°F$ ($15.5°C$). There must be good ventilation as air flow is an important factor when using an incubator, but no draught. Humidity is also an important factor to be considered; the optimum relative humidity should be around 50-60%. Incubators with a high air-flow rate need to be humid, therefore, if it is at all possible, site your incubator in an old outhouse or stable where the temperature does not fluctuate. The walls, if made of stone or brick will hold a certain amount of moisture which will help with humidity. It is well worth selecting the right spot.

### High Temperature

Always adjust your incubator before setting the eggs, however if the temperature remains higher than required, it could cause a nil hatch, but if only for a limited time it could result in some dead in shell. Unfortunately, the damage cannot be repaired, therefore that careful adjustment prior to incubation is all important.

### Low Temperature

This acts in the reverse to high temperature, depending on how low reflects the degree of delay in hatching taking place. However, this does not usually increase mortality, but the continual opening of the incubator - thus lowering the temperature - will give poor results; the same with candling the eggs too often, allowing the incubator to cool.

### Pre-heating of Eggs

It is best to allow your eggs to warm up over twentyfour hours before setting in the incubator and incubation starts, especially if the eggs have been stored for any length of time.

### Hatching by Incubator

Having completed the required incubation period, the chicks will hatch, usually in the case of Quail within a few hours of each other. This will mean there are chicks running between your remaining eggs in the incubator, so some people advise removing the chicks into another incubator set aside for hatching, to allow them to dry off. A chick does not require to eat for at least 24 hours as it will survive on the yolk sac absorbed prior to hatching.

## BROODER BOX

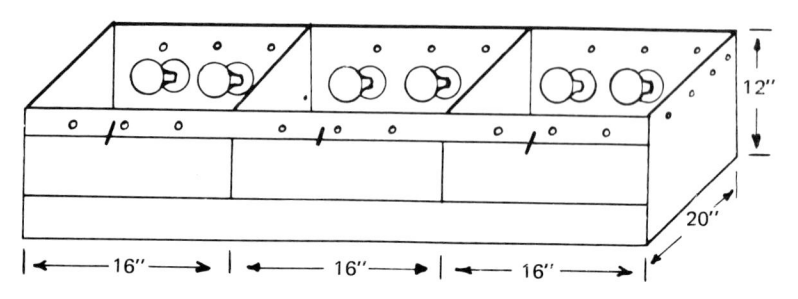

### Brooders

When your chicks are completely dry in the incubator, they can then be placed in a brooder box as illustrated. This is a box with an open top covered with small mesh wire netting, and an electric light bulb mounted on an adjustable base at the rear. You will see there are two bulbs to each compartment, as a safe guard in case one fuses. Normally the season starts with two 60 watt red or blue bulbs; to obtain the required temperature under the bulbs of 95°F (35°C), but as the ambient temperature rises during the season, one of the bulbs is replaced by a 5-8 watt Nite light, so light is still available, at the same time restricting heat.

## Floor Covering

There are a number of floor coverings which can be used. I favour corrugated paper for two reasons. First, the chicks can gain a secure foothold on the corrugations, and secondly, food can be sprinkled over the floor in front of the chicks and cannot be scattered into the corners, as with flat surfaces. Other people use rolled oats very successfully, which gives the chicks something to peck at and also a good foothold.

## Food and Water

For those raising the very small species of Quail, such as Chinese Painted Quail ( *E. chinensis* ), you must ensure that the food is ground small enough, and the water trough is not too large, thus preventing the chicks from drowning. The plastic fountain used for caged birds is ideal for the early days. Types of food and how much to feed is explained in Chapter 4.

## Brooding Temperature

At day-old stage, as already mentioned, the temperature should be around 95°F (35°C), this being reduced to about 85°F (29°C) after two weeks, when the chicks should be transferred to a larger brooder until they are fully feathered, and heat is required only at night. This is usually around 4-5 weeks of age.

## Alternative Types of Brooder

Some people prefer to use a black heat lamp of 150 watts which is hung over the chicks to give the required heat. The height from the ground for the correct temperature to be determined by trial and error. Additional light is also required, if natural light is not available. Always check that the black heat lamp is working, since no light is emitted from it.

## Transfer to the Outside

Only when your chicks have become fully fledged, and off the heat, should you consider placing them out of doors. It is as well to treat your young stock in the same way as adults at this stage, bearing in mind they will need a dry and draught-proof shelter to roost in at night.

At 10-12 weeks of age, the male birds will begin to show signs of their adult plumage, and it is at this time you should think about separating the sexes, if not, fighting or feather-pecking could well take place.

**Bantam Rearing of Quail**

Once the chicks have hatched, they should be placed in a coop with their mother, and given a diet of ground chick starter crumbs and clean water, again taking care the chicks do not drown. One method is to fill a shallow tray with water and place small stones in it, thus reducing the depth for them to fall in. A broody will take care of her chicks very well up to the stage when they are fully feathered, brooding them as and when required. They can be removed when independent of their mother.

## RELIABLE VISION INCUBATOR

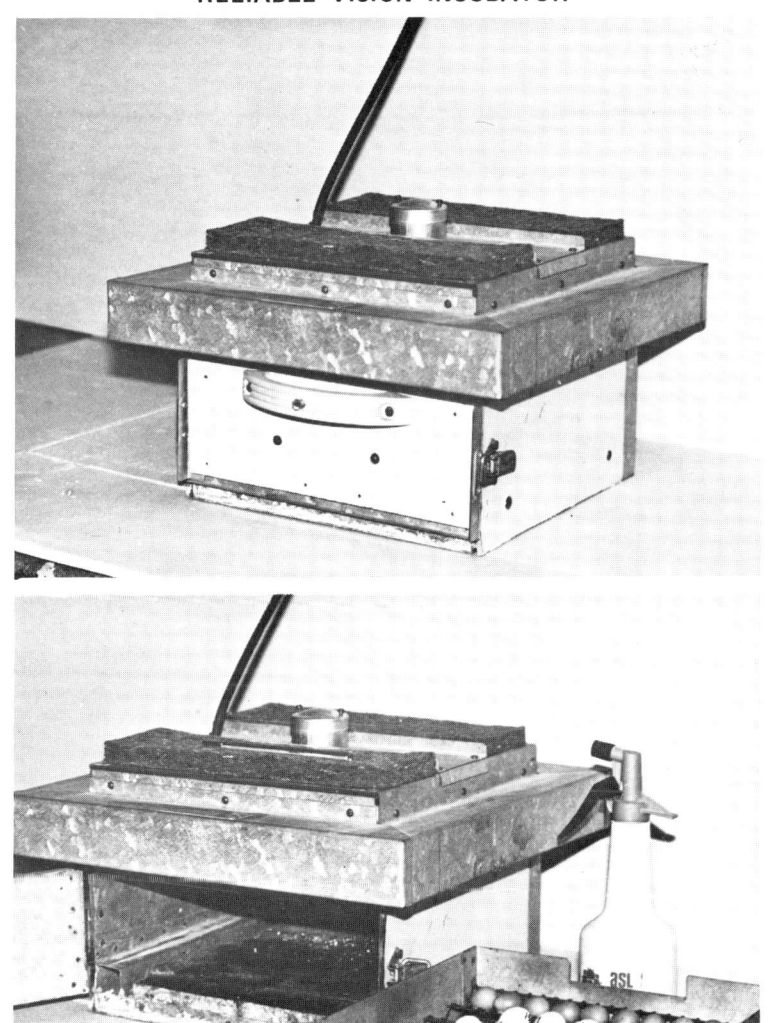

# FALCON CURFEW
## observation incubators

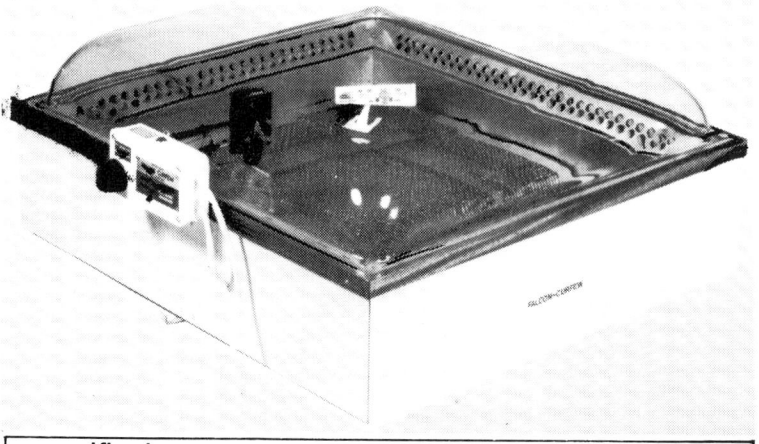

### specifications

**MAIN BODY** — Marine bonded water proof ply with full protective finish to resist both moisture and heat conditions.

**TOP** — "SEE THEM HATCH" moulded impact resistant heavy duty transparent plastic top with integral air outlet gives visibility with durability.

**INTERNAL PARTS** — Manufactured in prime galvanised steel for long rust free life.

**WATER TRAY** — Special design fitted with canvas humidity screen giving full moist air flow.

**HEATERS** — Arranged around all sides of the incubator in the full convection air flow, to give immediate response.

**HEAT CONTROL** — Extremely sensitive Microstat gives fine control.

**AIR INLET** — Adjustable for control of humidity and $CO_2$ content to give maximum hatches.

**EGG TRAY** — Galvanised steel and wire mesh covered with wide weave hessian to prevent chicks slipping.

**TOP COVER** — Bonded foam backed plastic to conserve heat and save hatching costs.

In common with all incubators, the Curfew is designed to raise normal room temperature. A cold site may cause excessive fuel consumption and/or temperature variation.

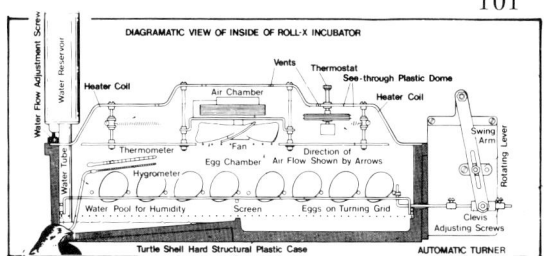

DIAGRAMATIC VIEW OF INSIDE OF ROLL-X INCUBATOR

# The ROLL-X INCUBATOR

by
**Marsh**

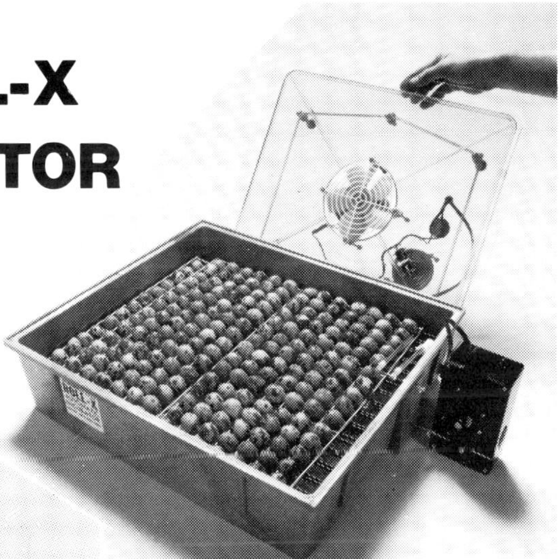

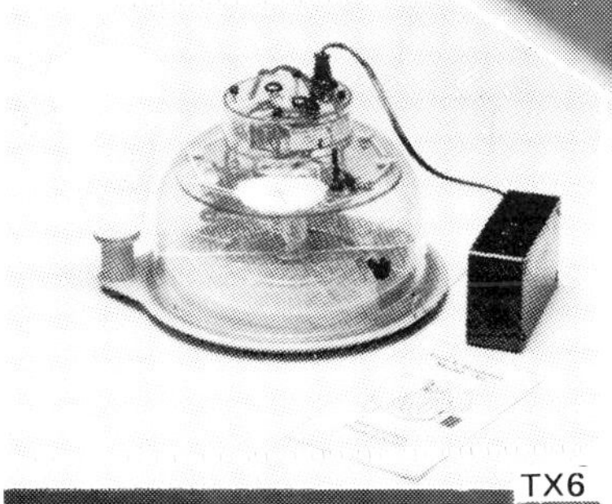

TX6

# *Turn-X Incubators*

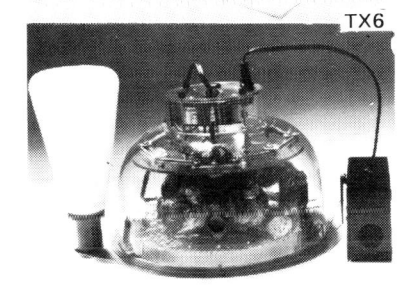

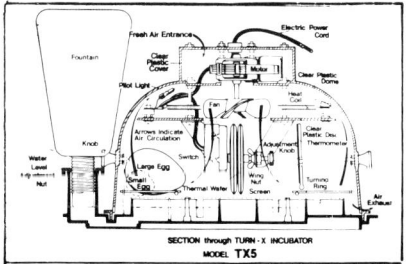

SECTION through TURN-X INCUBATOR MODEL **TX5**

# CHAPTER 7

## QUAIL AT LIBERTY

Once a breeder has formed a collection of quail, it is possible to consider releasing some birds to remain full-winged at liberty, using the presence of other birds to hold them in the vicinity. This, of course, is subject to certain conditions being available, such as no local cat to visit and disturb the birds, and your neighbours not objecting to the odd bird alighting in their garden and taking a quick nip at their lettuces in passing. Assuming you have the ideal conditions, the first step is to release a cock bird which has been well paired to a hen. In the early stages the hen bird must be visible to the cock when he is released. It is suggested he is separated from the hen and then allowed to walk quietly out into the open; this will allow him to obtain full details of his surroundings. Then, once he has found his way around the release area, and has a regular roost at night, in a tree or ideally in ivy on the side of the house, additional cock birds can be released. Unfortunately, should you release hen birds, they will pair and move out of the area. Always have food and water available away from vermin.

This system has been successfully used in one Surrey garden for at least two years running, with the birds weathering a hard winter with snow on the ground. There is nothing more charming to see than a Californian cock Quail strutting across a lawn in perfect feather, free to the world.

## CHAPTER 8

## IMPORTATION AND EXPORT OF QUAIL

Before anyone contemplates the importation of Galliformes from any part of the world, they must investigate the current legislation governing the movement of birds from one country to another, and the requirements differ between countries, as certain parts of the world are considered to be of a lower risk than others.

In the U.K. this information can be obtained from the Ministry of Agriculture and Fisheries, Animal Health Division, Government Buildings, Hook Rise, Tolworth, Surrey. These people will issue a health certificate for the birds you wish to export or issue the required licence to import into quarantine premises.

### Quarantine Premises

When considering the importation of birds, it must be clearly understood that if you consider offering quarantine facilities up for inspection, and they are near your own collection, the Ministry have the right to destroy all the birds on your premises should an imported bird be proven to have died from a notifiable disease. Assuming the above does not cause a problem, you may apply for details from the Ministry of Agriculture and Fisheries at the above address, and when you are ready they will send one of their officers to inspect your premises and issue a licence, either for a maximum of 12 birds for your own requirements, or a full quarantine licence covering as many birds as you wish. You will also need to consider a supply of young chickens which are used during the 35 days quarantine period as test birds, to establish if the imported birds are infected. Also during that period your local Vet will be required to visit each week and inspect the birds concerned. Fees are charged by the Ministry and your Vet for this service.

### Endangered Species

There are certain species of Quail on the protected list, and these are subject to importation under licence. The Ministry split them up into a number of categories: A (endangered species) B (vulnerable species) and as this list is amended from time to time, it would be well to apply to the Department of the Environment Wildlife Conservation Licencing Section, Tolgate House, Houlton St., Bristol BS2 9DJ.

### Transportation of Birds

There are very strict regulations governing the transport of birds by airlines and all shipments must comply with I.A.T.A. Regulations. These can be very involved and therefore guidance should be sought from WPA when required. However, there are some basic requirements. The shipper is responsible to see that the consignee's full name and address are clearly shown on the Air Waybill on each container, also to attach an I.A.T.A. Live Animals label on top correctly completed and the crate clearly marked "This Side Up" positioned on each corner.

### Shipping Documents

Apart from health certificates and licences and the Air Waybill which is completed by the carrier on behalf of the shipper, you will also be required to complete a Shippers Certification, which details all the basic information of the shipment; i.e. number of crates, description and quantity of birds, name and address of shipper, origin and destination.

### Feeding and Watering

During the course of a journey birds need to have both water and food. The standard crumb and millets are ideal, and chopped apples can provide an extra source of liquid. Water is likely to spill during transit, therefore if a piece of absorbent foam rubber is placed in the container this will help to conserve the supply.

### Containers

These must comply with the regulations laid down by I.A.T.A.

for the order of Galliformes shown on page 43 of the I.A.T.A. Live Animal Regulations (5th Edition June 1976) -

1): Materials - Burlap, Hardboard (Masonite), Plywood and Wood.
2): Design - For Quail
- a): each bird to be housed in an area to allow it to stand up and turn around comfortably.
- b): in the case of Quail, the container can be constructed of hardboard using 3.2 x 2cm (1.25 x 0.75 inches) wooden framing. The floor to be constructed of plywood, sides and roof of hardboard. Around the upper part of the sides 2.5cm (1 inch) ventilation holes are to be drilled equally spaced on all sides.
- c): No doors are necessary, one side can be unscrewed and removed to enable the birds to be placed inside, then repositioned and screwed up (indicating the side used).
- d): Food and water tins should fit into slots made in the front of the container and attached to the uprights of the framework so that they can be replenished without being removed.

NOTE: The foregoing must be regarded as guidance and not accepted as final. Therefore should an importation be considered seriously, you are well advised to contact the appropriate Ministry for the latest information before embarking on what can be a very expensive project.

# CHAPTER 9

## WORLD PHEASANT ASSOCIATION - QUAIL GROUP

### Membership of the WPA

This is open to all those in sympathy with the objects of the Association and willing to comply with its rules. WPA is an international organisation designed to enable all interested persons and institutions to participate in fulfilling the objectives of the Association. WPA is generally accepted as the most effective organisation for the conservation of the order of Galliformes in the world.

*Aims of the Quail Group within WPA.*
1): To bring together those who are interested in the keeping and breeding of captive Quail.
2): To encourage reserve collections and establish a breeding nucleus to ensure a viable breeding pool for the future.
3): To promote sound and improved methods of avicultural husbandry.
4): To assist and advise on the management of Quail in captivity.

### Advantages of Membership of WPA.

These include:-
1): Access to a data-bank of information on Quail and related birds.
2): Expert advice on all matters pertaining to aviculture of Quail and related birds.
3): Attending an Annual Conference in Great Britain or elsewhere.
4): The opportunity to visit various collections and conservation areas throughout the world.
5): An annual journal and three newsletters a year.

6): The opportunity to participate in special conservation programmes at home and overseas as determined by Council and Governments concerned.
7): Attendance at the AGM and participation in the election of officers in accordance with the Rules of the Association.
8): Other privileges as decided by the Council from time to time.

For subscription notes and further information, please write to:- The Administrator, WPA, Harraton Square, Church Lane, Exning, Suffolk. England. *Telephone:* Exning (063877) 717

# BIBLIOGRAPHY

Dr. A. F. Anderson Brown. *The Incubation Book.* Saiga Books. Hindhead, England.

Emmet. R. Blake. *Manual of Neotropical Birds*, Vol 1. University of Chicago Press, Chicago and London.

Edward. S. Gruson. *A Check-list of the Birds of the World*, 1976. Collins, London.

Paul A. Johnsgard. *Grouse and Quail of North America.* University of Nebraska, Lincoln, U.S.A.

A. Rutgers and K. A. Norris. *Encyclopoedia of Aviculture*, Vol. 1. Blandford Press, London.